Children's Ministry

in a Digital Age

By Dr. Innocent Ononiwu

Children's Ministry in a Digital Age

Trilogy Christian Publishers A Wholly Owned Subsidary of Trinity Broadcasting Network

2442 Michelle Drive Tustin, CA 92780

Cover design by: Adaeze Opara

Library of Congress Cataloging-in-Publication Data is available.

ISBN: 978-1-63769-840-2

E-ISBN: 978-1-63769-841-9

"'Children's Ministry in a Digital Age' by Dr. Innocent On-oniwu is a gold mine of truth and an invaluable treasure to anyone involved in children's ministry in this generation. The author is one of the key men God has used for more than forty years to shape young people's minds and lives from Nigeria to the United States of America and beyond. I was particularly taken in by the author's narrative on the importance of the Holy Spirit in impacting our young ones in these last days. I regard Him (the Holy Spirit) as the secret source of success in children's evangelistic ministry. This book is a classic that comes well recommended."

— Dr. Sola Osundeko (MD)
Senior Pastor RCCG York, Pennsylvania

"The Fruit: The writings in this book are what I would like to call a testimony. Truly, throughout the book are examples, like mine, of changed lives.

"I met Innocent in 1978, as we arrived at the University of Ife (currently OAU) in Ile-Ife from the United States. We joined the All Souls Chapel, which had a vibrant children's ministry run by Innocent Ononiwu and Nathaniel Nwankpa. This group of serious biblical students came from the Evangelical Christian Union. Approximately a month later, our children came home with such enthusiasm and excitement over their time in the children's ministry. This prompted me to go and see what was happening there! I met Innocent and Nathaniel and had several encounters with the children.

"The All Souls Chapel Children's Ministry's activity group was known as the Happiness Club. Our children are Manita Fadel (Soremekun) and Morenike Ogebe (Soremekun). Certainly, through this foundation-laying experience, our children came

3

to know the Lord in an unforgettable way. It laid the basis for their accepting the Lord as their Personal Savior in the 1980s in the USA.

"The Happiness Club not only changed my children's lives, but also my own. I became an avid parent as I also worked with the women in All Souls Chapel 1979-1983. These experiences paved the way for a full-time ministry involving the teaching and preaching of God's word. The 'Fruit' of Happiness Club is quite vast."

—Dr. Elizabeth Soremekun, PhD
Director, Highlands Education International School,
and Pastor, Mountain Top Family Worship,
Gembu, Taraba State, Nigeria

"Children's Ministry in a Digital Age is a wake-up call for children's ministers to be sensitive to the needs of children in a digital age and evolve a relevant and pragmatic approach to engage them with the gospel. The call to reach the child with the gospel has not changed; what has changed over the years are the methods of teaching. These changes in approach are inevitable because of the peculiarities of each era. Dr. Innocent Ononiwu is a veteran Children's Minister and a lover of children. The first time I met him was in the late '70s, teaching children at All Souls Chapel, University of Ife (Nigeria). He was a leader in children's ministry at a time when children's ministry was not well known in Nigeria. This book is a must for every children's ministry worker or

4

parent who wants to succeed in the task of raising and mold-
ing lives for God in a digital age. Having been at the fore-
front of evangelizing children for more than four decades, I
can boldly declare that this book will be of great benefit to
the body of Christ."

—Evang. Egbuna Tony Chukwudile
President, Children Evangelism Ministry Int'l

"This book has so many hidden treasures for those who
are prayerfully stepping into the calling of children's minis-
try. The presence and teaching of the Holy Spirit are so vital
in rooting and anchoring the next generation—to help ush-
er them into their God-ordained purpose and destiny. The
author has shown that when we walk in the guidance and
power of the Holy Spirit, we are unlimited in what we can do
for the Kingdom of God! I do love the personal stories—the
victories and the failures—both are great teachers in life.
Doing great work for the Kingdom does not have to be com-
plicated but rather simple - minister the whole truth of God's
word. Thank you, Dr. Innocent, for your obedience in shar-
ing your wisdom, insight, and practical knowledge that the
Holy Spirit has taught you and your wife, Vickie, along the
way. Continue to stay in your lane!"

—Angeline Posey
Director of Youth Ministry CEIC Chesapeake, Virginia

"To stay current and connected to the children in our care, we must make the extra effort to understand their world. One way to do so is to keep abreast with technology. That is their language. They are the digital natives."

—Dr. Innocent Ononiwu

Dedication

To the Lord most high.

To my wife, Vickie, and to our children: Chiagozie, Chibuzo, Chidiuto, Chiemika and Chiedozie.

To all teachers, who work to show the children the way they should go.

Acknowledgments

My thanks go to all the teachers who work in the background, training the children in our Sunday schools, children's ministries, and gospel clubs. You are the unsung heroes who shape the future of our children. I am especially grateful to all of you that I have been privileged to work with in nearly half a century of ministry to children. Without you, I could not have done much. I am indebted to the parents who have consistently worked with us to fulfill our God-given mandate to feed the lamb. God bless you all.

Most of the original editing of the manuscript was done by our beloved sister Tani Ifediora, the author of *Buds Blossom and Bloom*. I owe her a debt of gratitude. Further editing and proofreading were carried out by our son-in-law Joseph Cobb and our daughter Chidiuto Cobb, and I am grateful to them. Judith Musau, one of the teachers in our current church, and Dr. Manita Fadel, the First Lady of RCCG North America, read through the manuscript and made valuable suggestions for which I am thankful. Angeline Posey, Candace Carr, Dr. Kemi Ogunsan, and Dr. Wande Oguntoyinbo are seasoned children and youth ministers who suggested some topics that I discussed in this book. Thank you.

Final editing and proofreading of this book before I sent it to the publisher were done by my wife, Vickie, a literary critic and current head of our church's adult Sunday school department. Cherie, you are a blessing to me. Thank you. Pastor Sola Osundeko (MD), the senior pastor of RCCG York, and his wife, Pastor Teni Osundeko (PhD), have been supportive of our children's ministry and have been pillars of encouragement to us since we joined the church. I am grateful.

It is a great honor to have Dr. Tracey Jones, the president of Tremendous Leadership, author of eight books, air force veteran, and a much-sought-after international speaker on leadership, accept to write the foreword to this book. Getting to know Dr. Jones and her husband, Mike, has been a blessing to me. I also thank evangelist Egbuna Chukwudile, the president of Children Evangelism Ministry, who has been my co-laborer in the children's ministry for more than forty years; Dr. Elizabeth Soremekun, my co-Sunday school teacher in the late seventies, Angeline Posey, Director of the youth ministry at CEIC in Chesapeake, Virginia, and Pastor Sola Osundeko for writing reviews on this book.

Finally, I am grateful to the "children" we have been privileged to teach all these years, who still keep in touch with us. I am most grateful to those who have shared their reflections of the impact of our programs on their lives, careers, and ministries; Dr. Paul Aliu, Pastor Yemi Adeyemo, Dr. Nnenna Ugoji, His Lordship Lenu Apapa, Chidiuto Cobb JD, Kelechi Eluchie, Engineer Nonso Ude, Nosa Lawani, Olayemi Fadahunsi, and Abigail Musau. You are the reason we have stayed on our beat this long. God bless you all.

My niece, Adaeze Opara, created the front cover design for this book. My thanks to her. I am grateful to the Lord for such a gift.

Table of Contents

Foreword

I was a lifelong Christian well into my middle-age years before I truly understood the baptism of the Holy Spirit. I spent decades of my youth and early adulthood taught but not trained in how to integrate faith into every aspect of my life. And we wonder why so many of our young people spend years failing to launch in their faith or walking away completely. Dr. Innocent's book takes on the biggest mistake we have made in discipling our children, assuming they are too young to comprehend and experience the infusion of the Holy Spirit. This book is essential for all of us, not just those in children's ministry. We must, as a body, protect and raise the most tender and vulnerable in our society. Children's ministry is not a daycare and must be constructed and executed in a way that unfolds our future leaders. Dr. Innocent takes you through every age group of youth and explains how to best introduce them to the power and personhood of the Holy Spirit. This is a powerful read that will completely change the way you look at a children's ministry and awaken you to how instrumental it is in raising our youth in the church age.

—Dr. Tracey Jones MBA, PhD
President Tremendous Leadership

Preface

I have had the desire to write a book that would document some of our field experiences working with children for nearly half a century. During the lockdown because of the coronavirus pandemic, I did not have any excuse to postpone it any longer. For a journey that started in 1972, I have been privileged to weather through several seasons of the evolution of children's ministry in two different continents. I have seen firsthand the struggles that churches and ministries experience, recruiting quality and goal-oriented teachers in Sunday schools. I have also seen the efforts that some teachers put into the ministry without much help from the church leadership team. One sad observation I have made over the years is that some teachers put in time and effort, yet the outcome often is nowhere commensurate with the input. Most children who go through our Sunday schools do not turn out the way they ought to. We need to do more. In this book, we have outlined what we need to do and how we need to give the Holy Spirit His seat in our children's ministry if we are looking for great results. This is fundamental. Unfortunately, not much emphasis is given to the work of the Holy Spirit in Children's ministries.

Contemporary children's ministry must take into account the digital revolution that has permeated the fabrics of our societies in the past few decades. Children's teachers need to adopt technology to be able to minister effectively to the children. We explored technology best practices that will help us identify and understand the needs of the children in our care. Since we could not accommodate the vast resources available to teachers in this book, we have provided links and references at the end of the book to help teachers source for more information and resources.

Our prayer and hope are that every teacher or parent who reads this book will find nuggets of wisdom that will help them prosper in the ministry and assignments that God has given them. If, by the end of the day, you find one piece of information in this book that makes your outreach and grooming of the children more effective, we will consider this effort worthwhile and a success. Please share this with other teachers, parents, pastors, and members of your church/ministry leadership team.

God's rich blessings.

Innocent Ononiwu, PhD

Introduction

There are many advantages of the internet and the media. Properly harnessed, these are powerful tools for good. However, unlike any other time in history, these are times when information from the internet, television, video games, radio, school, and peer groups inundate and saturate the environment in which the children who walk through the doors of our Sunday schools, gospel clubs, and children's churches live and grow up. Unfortunately, many are fully exposed to a forest of ungodly information from these sources. Most of the information that they are saturated with runs counter to what we, as children's ministry teachers, parents, and responsible adults, really want them to be exposed to at their young ages. We are faced with the challenge of bringing the children up the way they should go, as we have been commanded to do in the scriptures. Let us face it: the competing interests for their attention and interest is a war targeting their very souls and lives.

Not only is the array of information wide, but it is also continuous in a never-ceasing daily bombardment. The Sunday school teachers and minders have only a few hours (two to three), once a week, of interaction with these young ones. The question now is, how do we successfully undo the six-day mess the week has crammed into their lives? Not long ago, I spent the weekend preparing the lesson for my pre-teen Sunday school class. We were doing a series on faith, and I had my lesson plan ready to go. As I started my discussion on faith, I noticed that a twelve-year-old boy was having a sidebar with other children, talking about astral projections. I was shocked by the subject and was speechless for a moment, utterly unprepared for the tackle. Where did he draw this knowledge from? Curious, I probed some more, and what I discovered numbed me. Right under my nose, some of the children were consuming satanic literature, videos, and commentaries. The situation was urgent. I put aside my lesson plan for the day and focused the topic on demons and their operations, strictly from the scriptures. We followed up the teaching with prayers of deliverance.

Studies have shown that by age thirteen, most children assume that they have learned everything they ought to know about the Bible. This presumably would be correct if all that the Bible offered was the story of Jonah and the big fish, Noah and the Ark, Moses and the Red Sea, David and Goliath, Samson and Delilah, etc. They would be correct if the foundational instructions of being nice to people, obeying parents, giving offerings and tithes, and generally being a good "Samaritan" were the be-all and end-all. Why would they need to know more beyond memorizing Psalm 23, the Lord's prayer, a spattering of weekly memory verses and adorned in this weak armor, be expected to face the formidable arsenal of an unrelenting foe? Every form of surreptitious evil is strained through the colors and music of the entertainment industry, which has become, so to speak, a veritable recruitment agency for hell. The children are enticed and lured by the flashing colors of sin embedded in these forms of entertainment into lives of immorality and violence. They are powerless until we equip them with counter-narratives and Scriptures that will help them to stand against the hosts of demons that they contend with.

As teachers and children's ministers, we need to wake up, peel open our eyes (physical and spiritual), and sit up! What responses do we have when the children in our care are expanding their horizons in the knowledge of the occult and immorality right under our noses? How much do we care about their spiritual health? How much do we teach them about the Holy Spirit these days and practically lead them into the supernatural experience of the baptism of the

Holy Spirit and enduement with power? Oh, have we experienced these ourselves? You cannot give what you do not have. Some may believe that children are not mature enough to understand the person and ministry of the Holy Spirit. Indeed, children's church curricula, books, and programs fail to mention the Holy Spirit. Little wonder that many children who spend their formative years in our children's assemblies are so ill-equipped that they end up slipping in their teenage years and totter towards new age religions on getting into the universities and colleges.

Let me share a personal story here. One Sunday in the mid-eighties, I was teaching my pre-teen and teenagers' class in our children's Sunday school at All Souls Chapel, University of Ife in Nigeria, and it was time for our annual review of the topics we covered during the year. After the review, I asked the children what subjects they would want us to address in the coming year. One child answered by asking a question which came to me as a surprise. "Uncle, why don't you teach us about the Holy Spirit?" she asked. Another one echoed her question, "Yes, Uncle, why don't you teach us about the Holy Spirit?" Their responses came to me as a rebuke from the Lord. In ten years of teaching these children in Sunday school, not once had I ever taken the time to present to them the person and ministry of the Holy Spirit. Why? First, the subject was not in the curriculum we followed, and second, somewhere in my mind, I had decided that it was an "advanced" part of ministry and not for children. Of course, I was wrong. We must put away such unfortunate thinking, which will only leave our children vulnerable to the evil one. We live in dire times, and it is imperative to ensure that children are grounded in the knowledge of the person and work of the Holy Spirit.

Consider that these extremely cute, well brought up children are regaling on video games with virtual friends in Australia, China, South Africa, India, or wherever. These playmates become their buddies, with each having unfettered access to the other's thinking processes. Without being awake in the Spirit, our children are sitting ducks to be seduced and recruited into a panoply of godless philosophies and demonic religions. It is high time we planted the right seed into them that they may walk sure, confident in the power of the Holy Spirit and authority in the name of Jesus. It bears repeating here; we need the Holy Spirit in the lives of the children entrusted to our care. We need Him to guard and direct them. If our children can talk about astral travels, why can't they freely and authoritatively talk about the word of knowledge, word of wisdom, discerning of spirits, or prophecy? Why can't they talk about an experience when they *heard* the Lord speak to them and give them specific instructions? Why is worship limited to musical entertainment and not a supernatural experience? In this digital age, have we completely lost the sense of the supernatural?

Please come along. Let us explore these issues and more as we prepare to lead our children into the glorious experience of the supernatural.

1

Understanding the Call

The Challenge

Children's ministries all over the world have the sin-gular privilege of molding the lives of the next generation and shaping them for an enviable eternity. We have been entrusted with a sacred duty to train up a child the way he should go. It is a responsibility that we cannot take lightly. Our charge *is* not to entertain the children or take them through a western cultural experience where, later in life, the child will point back to Easter eggs and bunnies, Hallelujah nights, and Santa Claus coming down the chimney to fulfill

25

their gift list wishes. A lot of time and resources are being spent on things that have no eternal value, which distract and draw away from the truth. The call is to *train* the children in the *way* they *should go*. There is only one *way* they should go, and that is the way that leads to the One who said, "I am the *way*, the truth and the life"—Jesus Christ. Therefore, no matter the curriculum, activity, or experience - if not designed to lead them in the *way* they should go, it is a complete waste of resources. Any program that is not Christ-centered is merely social entertainment. Children's ministers have only one job description—to "train up a child the way he should go"—any deviation from this job description does not earn any reward. A deviation may warrant stern, corrective actions.

Studies have shown that 60-70 percent of young adults drop out of church when they go to college[1]. More than seven out of ten of these young adults say that they did not intend to leave the church but simply drifted off. Why? They did not have a significant attachment to the church. There was no commitment to Christianity. They were not rooted in Christ and therefore were very vulnerable to the winds of new age philosophies and doctrines of men. The stories they learned in Children's Sunday school were simply stories that did not translate to eternal spiritual victuals for the journey of life. They did not have the spiritual backbones that would stand the slightest push. Their teachers probably taught them the best they knew how but did not go the extra mile to model Christianity to them. I can picture some of these children feeling the emotions that Becky Fisher, the author of *Redefining Children's Ministry in the Twenty-First Century,* felt about the endless stories we tell the children in our classes without transitioning the stories into tools for positive spiritual engagement.

Becky writes,

> My father was a pastor, so I was one of those children who cut their teeth on the proverbial church pew. I had been in church all my life. I loved it, and I loved the Lord. We were blessed to have one of the best children's ministers of the day in our church. But at about twelve years of age, I distinctly remember sitting in one of our kid's services thinking; *If I hear the story of David and Goliath one more time, I'm going to scream!*[2]

There are many pre-teen Becky Fishers out there in our children's churches and ministries that are screaming inside and exploding with frustration about the monotonous spiritual meals that we feed them every Sunday. Have you tried eating your favorite meal three times a day for one week? If you have not, let me describe the feeling for you. As a young pharmacist, I was posted to a city in Nigeria called Bauchi to serve my country in the National Youth Service Corps scheme. This is a mandatory one-year service for college and university graduates in Nigeria who are under thirty years of age. Bauchi state was in dire need of doctors and pharmacists. The state government did everything possible to make these professionals comfortable. When I arrived at my primary place of service, the hospital that I was posted to had just given out the last house available in the staff quarters to a couple (both doctors) that they had hired. They made a "temporary" arrangement and got me accommodation in one of the topmost hotels in the city. I enjoyed the stay in the hotel; the meals were great, and my suite was very peaceful. The sheets were changed often, and I did not bother much with laundry. I spent a lot of time after work writing poems and songs and developing my drawing skills.

All was great at the beginning. However, I did not know that the state would keep me there for ten months, all expenses paid. I was even entitled to three guests per meal at the state's expense. It got to a point when I literally hated going to the hotel's restaurant to eat. The thought of going for breakfast, lunch, or dinner was nauseating. My meals were limited to what the hotel served, and there was not much variety. I ate almost the same thing for breakfast every day. The choices for lunch and dinner were the same menu every day for ten months. On occasions, I would invite one

28

or two of my Youth Corps friends to share meals with me at the hotel in exchange for going to their apartments to eat something else not served at the hotel. I needed a variety of foods. In a similar way, the children under our care need a regular variety of spiritual diets. They need spiritual cereals, pasta, vegetables, meat, etc. They need proteins, carbohydrates, minerals, and vitamins. In other words, they need a variety of balanced spiritual diets. Unfortunately, most of their teachers are stuck in gear one all year round. Teachers follow curricula that are designed to teach just morals and Bible stories and little else. Meanwhile, non-Christian authors and movie producers are pushing the envelope and exposing the children to horror movies and books. Why are they so creative, bold, and successful in promoting their godless agenda, and we are so timid about teaching the children about supernatural experiences available to Christians? I believe the simple answer is that many of the teachers have not experienced the supernatural. Thus, they are unable to give what they do not have.

The explosion of technology in the past three decades has introduced challenges that the children's church teacher must confront to effectively communicate with the children under his/her care. It is like everyone is constantly learning new ways to adapt to emerging technologies. No sooner have you learned how to use a particular technology than another one emerges from the creative minds of scientists and engineers. This renders your knowledge obsolete. Take, for example, the evolution of video recording devices. There was a time when only television stations had the capabilities and technical know-how to do video recordings. It is all different now. In 1988 I did a video documentary of the activities of Happiness Club, the activity arm of our children's Sunday school. My brother had one of the best video cameras and editing suites in Nigeria at that time. These were big cameras that were operated by well-trained technicians. The reels for the tapes were equally big. Fast forward to 2006, I did another documentary in Maryland (USA), and the cameramen had powerful recorders, which they held with one hand. These small recorders produced high-definition quality images. Now, almost everyone you meet on the street has a multi-functional gadget in their pockets called cell phones which have powerful video recorders. The quality of the pictures produced by these phones was unimaginable a few years back, and the speed of sharing video files is nothing that we could have contemplated a couple of years ago. Technology changes constantly, and the younger ones adapt much faster than their teachers.

For all its versatile utility, the cell phone is one piece of technology that the teacher must deal with almost every Sunday. For one, it is a personal property, and there is a limit to which you can stop the owner from using it without infringing on their constitutional rights. Also, most children have their Bible apps on their phones. However, it is a major source of distraction for the children as they switch back and forth from browsing the internet, chatting on social media, playing games, and paying attention to classroom instructions. The cell phone is like an extension of their hands. They tend to react badly if you deny them the use of their phones, even if it is for a brief period. For effective class management, the teacher must find a way to control the use of cell phones in his class.

Like I said earlier, children are almost always faster at adopting new technologies than their teachers. There is a generational divide in catching up with technology. Generation D seems to do better with current technology than generation C, and generation C is more technologically savvy than generation B, etc.

Recently a church member donated large screen smart television sets to our children's church. I thought that I was sufficiently good with technology, especially as I used it a lot to teach my web-enhanced classes in the university. I decided to set up one of the television sets for my class in the full glare of my nine to twelve-year-old Sunday school pupils. That was a huge mistake. Midway, I got stuck. The remote control was so different from any that I had ever used or seen, and most of the set-up depended on it. I tried all sorts of options (including reading the manual), but nothing seemed to work in the heat of the moment. Meanwhile, I had announced to the class that we were going to watch a Christian movie, and the children were waiting. The children watched me in abated amusement as I struggled with the puzzle this new technology posed. After what seemed like an eternity of embarrassment, trying to figure out this technological riddle, I gave up. I swallowed my pride and tried to get some help from our technical team. However, there was a problem; the technical team was in the main sanctuary and we were in the church basement. It was praise and worship time in the sanctuary, and I would have to wait until it was over to speak with the person that I felt was knowledgeable enough to fix the problem. It was at this point that one of the children offered to help. The twelve-year-old said, "Dr. Innocent, can I help?" I said, "Yes." Help from anyone was most welcome at this point. She took the remote control, pressed one or two buttons, and in less than ten seconds, we were on our way. Problem solved! I felt very ancient at that moment.

To stay current and connected to the children in our care, we must make the extra effort to understand their world. One way to do so is to keep abreast with technology. That is their language. They are the digital natives. Communication gets harder when you do not understand someone's language and culture. Consider sharing your good news with a Japanese man who does not understand a word of English. Is it frustrating? It cannot be otherwise. No matter how excited you are, your joy is limited if you cannot share it with a friend simply because of a language barrier. In the same way, you are unable to share the good news effectively with children in your class if you have difficulty expressing yourself in their language—technology. They were born during the digital revolution that started in the seventies and exploded at the turn of this millennium. Technology is their mother tongue. It is ingrained in their social DNA. The older generation does not have a choice but to keep pace with them and always stay ahead of the curve.

The Dilemma

Before we get into discussing the assignment that God has given us concerning the training of children, let us clear a little dilemma that most teachers struggle with. Most of us are volunteers in the children's ministry. In other words, we believe that we are called to satisfy a need. In all the many years that I have served the Lord in children's ministry, I have not seen any teacher who is paid to take care of the children in our children's churches and ministries. If you receive a salary, God bless you. You need to take the assignment twice as seriously as I do, and if you know how seriously I take it, you have a lot of work on your shoulders. The point here is that some of us are specifically called by the Lord into this ministry, and we know it. Others are requested to do it by someone else, like the pastor or an elder in the church. Another group of volunteers calls themselves into the ministry. It may be that they like working with children or simply like solving problems by volunteering where the need is. Almost all of us are volunteers. Whichever route you took to get into the children's ministry, you have work to do, and understanding the assignment is a responsible place to start from.

What is your idea of a children's ministry? Is it a daycare or a garden where you sow seeds that have eternal value? Do not be in haste to tell me that it is the latter because that is not the total picture. It is both a daycare and a garden. You cannot be effective as a teacher if your view of the assignment is lopsided. When I came to the United States in 2002, I attended a church where the children's department was called "daycare." On that day, the adults and children had the praise and worship time together in the sanctuary. After the worship, the senior pastor announced that the children should go to the daycare. I got curious. I wanted to know what they did at the daycare. I followed the children and their teachers. A cursory evaluation of what I saw going on helped me to understand why God took me to that church. My original plan was to attend another church. Rather, I settled down in this church and gradually worked with the children's Sunday school superintendent. First, we worked to let the church leadership and the teachers know that we were dealing with something bigger than babysitting the children.

Second, we changed the name from daycare to the children's Sunday school department. By the time we left the city four years later, the entire orientation and focus of the children's ministry in this church had changed completely till this day.

The leadership of most churches sees the children's ministry as a daycare where the teachers babysit the children to allow their parents some space to receive the Word without being disturbed by the cry of their babies or any distractions from their children. Tragically, many teachers also go with the same mindset, and that is reflected in the level of commitment they display. They see the children's ministry as a crèche where babies and young children are cared for by relief volunteers. They play songs, show cartoons, and tell the children stories, enough to keep them engaged till their parents are done worshipping the Lord. Children who go through this *cultural Christianity* in the children's ministry end up looking elsewhere for spiritual fulfillment when they become teenagers or young adults. In addition to looking after the children while their parents worship in the sanctuary, every children's ministry teacher must recognize that there is a higher calling. God Himself has called you to a noble purpose. He has called you as a partner with him to train each child under your care the way he/she *should* go. He wants each one of them to go through a *committed Christian* experience. It is a big responsibility. Once we recognize the huge responsibility that God has placed on our shoulders, we

35

shall treat the children's ministry with a different attitude. I was only sixteen years old when I had a clear revelation that this is God's purpose for my life. By God's grace, I have tried to remain focused on this vision for almost fifty years. I keep learning every day how to stay on this lane without changing my course.

Some senior pastors of the churches that I attended have asked to make me a pastor, and one has called from another church to offer me a position to pastor a branch of his church. As honorable as the position of a pastor is, I have consistently declined the offers. One of my pastors wanted so much to make me a pastor in his church that when I repeatedly declined his offers, he continued to call me Pastor Innocent. He then gave me an office as the children's church coordinator and put a label on the door which read "Children's Church Pastor." To put that matter to rest, the Lord did something interesting. Both of us were scheduled to pray together in the church one day, and just before we started, a pastor called and told him that she was on her way to our church. She wanted to check out the carpet we used for our church. I did not know the lady before then. My pastor introduced her as a pastor and that she had served the Lord for more than forty-five years smuggling Bibles into communist countries. He then told the pastor that we just came to pray together and requested her to pray for me. She obliged. For whatever reason, she laid her hands on my head to pray and quickly withdrew them as if she were jolted by an electric shock. She started prophesying instead. One of the things she said in the prophecy was that I should continue in the ministry that God gave me. I should remain focused. She said that some people would want to give me titles and change my course but that I should not change my lane. After that prophecy from a stranger, our pastor never broached the issue of being ordained a pastor with me again. If God has called you to be a pastor in a church denomination, please go ahead and be ordained. I know what my calling is. The calling to raise children for the kingdom of God is the best job anybody can have on this earth. We must deliver the goods because the Holy Spirit stands ready to do his work once we introduce Him to the children. Yes, we shall babysit the children, but the nobler goal is to train them to become committed Christians all the days of their lives.

Training, Teaching, and Lecturing

Have you ever wondered how pharmacists remember the names, actions, and side effects of so many drugs belonging to different therapeutic classes? The answer is that we are *trained* to do so. It is brick by brick, classes after classes and labs after labs. By the time one goes through the course sequence, each drug class has become part of your waking breath. We cannot afford to make mistakes. If an architect makes a mistake in the design of a house, he can either live with it or fix it. But if a pharmacist or a doctor makes a mistake, he may end up burying his patient. Quite often, the pharmacist is the last contact between a drug and a patient. Our training demands rigor. There is a course in my Pharmacy school days in which any score less than 90 percent was a failure. If you scored 89 percent and protested to your professor or asked him to round it off to 90 percent, he would promptly remind you that you just killed a patient and therefore deserved a failure. That sounds harsh, but that is the reality. In real life, if you dispense a blood thinner (an anticoagulant) instead of a pain medication, your patient may bleed to death. It is not good enough to say, "Oh, it was just a medication error." The consequence of the error is huge. That is why the training is rigorous. In a similar way, a mistake by a Sunday school teacher may be costly. It can drive a child away from church for the rest of his life. You cannot afford to take children's ministry lightly.

I get fascinated watching Simone Biles, the most decorated American gymnast who, at the time of writing this book, has won thirty gold medals in the Olympics and world championships. Her flexibility, agility, and speed thrill me to no ends. However, her balance beam skills keep me on edge. Whether it is her front and back walkovers, split leaps, front and back handsprings, or saltos, especially the triple salto, I find myself instinctively praying for her. While I am almost having a heart attack watching her perform some of those incredible hair-splitting routines being shown on television, they are probably nothing to her. The reason she does them effortlessly is because of years of constant training. We are called to train the children and not to lecture them. There is a clear distinction between giving a lecture, teaching, and training. In a simplified form, the differences lie in the level of involvement of the person delivering the instruction to the learning process. Of the three instructional methods, lecturing is the most far removed from the student's learning process. A *lecturer* comes to the class, gives the students the outline of what they are supposed to know, provides the references, and gives a brief overview of the subject matter, and his work is done. A *teacher* goes into greater detail to explain the subject to the student. He comes up with creative ways of passing the information to his student. He is more invested in the student understanding and retaining the subject that he teaches than the lecturer. A *trainer's* involvement in the student's learning process is more intense. He is more of a hands-on teacher. He is a coach, a role model, and a mentor. He considers a student's success or failure his personal success or failure. He does all the work of a teacher and more. He watches the student apply the principles he is taught. He watches him make mistakes and corrects him. At times he asks the student to watch him as he carries out the task by himself. He then makes the student repeat the process several times under his supervision until he is satisfied that his student can do it all by himself. He develops a bond with his students, which at times becomes a lifetime mentoring relationship. Trainers invest their lives in the trainees. In the process, they replicate themselves.

That is what our Lord Jesus Christ did with the twelve disciples. He taught them, mentored them, and modeled life for them. He sent them out for their practicum, and they brought back reports of the miracles that they performed in His name. After He ascended into heaven, His disciples carried on the work here on earth, having been *trained* by the Master. That band of twelve disciples turned the world upside down to His glory. We are called to be trainers and not just teachers or lecturers to the children in our care.

Unfortunately, we spend so much time *teaching* or *lecturing* the children but barely any time *training* them by comparison. That is the crux of the matter. Some of our children's Sunday schools are like traditional online classes where both the instructors and the students are faceless and, in a hurry, to complete the curriculum. We simply download what the curriculum says that we should teach and present to the children in less than two hours of interaction every Sunday. They are not graduate students who can work independently to understand concepts. Even graduate students need direction and, in many cases, *training*. Imagine what happens if a student pilot receives two hours of instructions on *how to* fly an airplane every week but never gets to fly the airplane with an instructor by his side. Most of the worst drivers we see on the road are those who "taught" themselves to drive. There are basic rules for driving safely on the road. That is why responsible governments require a minimum number of hours of hands-on driving with an instructor by the side of the student driver. People who circumvent these standards end up learning their lessons the hard way. In a similar way, we are called to train the children and not just to teach or lecture them. If we do not train them the way they should go, they find other ways and make a shipwreck of their lives.

2

The Sunday School Teacher's Credentials

You are a teacher: are you qualified?

There is a reason why there are accrediting bodies that independently evaluate the environment, programs, and academic credentials of teachers and educational institutions before any institution is approved to train students and award diplomas. It is to maintain minimum standards. Some institutions that are well–endowed may have additional expertise or history that gives them the edge over less privileged schools, but a standard curriculum and standardized tests ensure that students meet minimum standards before they are released into the world, irrespective of what schools they attend or their zip codes. The situation is different in churches. We do not require teachers to have specific academic qualifications or certificates before they are approved to teach in children's ministries. In most churches, the children's teachers are not professional teachers and do not have the academic qualifications to teach. They are just volunteers who feel a *calling* to minister to children. On the other hand, many of the professional teachers in churches may feel a calling in other areas of ministry other than teaching children. For example, they may feel more calling as prayer warriors or ushers and will perform excellently well at these stations than they would if asked to teach in children's Sunday school. When calling meets professional qualification, there is often a synergy that boosts the performance of such teachers. Training volunteer teachers is very much needed in our children's ministries because we are dealing with precious lives. However, there are basic credentials that every teacher in the children's ministry must have.

Are you born again?

My nephew Chijioke Ononiwu had a way of embarrassing my brother's guests when he was about three years old. He would simply ask them an unexpected question. "Uncle, are you born again?" he would ask and innocently wait for an answer. You better be born again, or you would be forced to tell this innocent child a lie. Let me borrow the question from Chijioke and ask you without mincing words. "Are you born again?" This is the major requirement for anybody to teach in the children's church or Sunday school. If you are not born again, you do not have the spiritual qualification to teach in the children's church. Forgive me if I am blunt. You are spiritually blind, and there is no way you can lead the spiritually sighted. That will not be consistent with reality. It is the sighted who leads the blind and not the other way around. Teaching children is a spiritual undertaking. If you are not equipped spiritually, you are treading on a dangerous turf. For one thing, the devil knows your spiritual status and knows what to do with you. He can frustrate and embarrass you or otherwise recruit you as an agent to propagate his agenda in the children's church. If it is the latter, you are even in a more dangerous position because you will be working against God. Here is the danger that you face and the warning which has been clearly spelled out in the scriptures, "Whoever causes one of these little ones who believe in me to sin, it would be better for him if a millstone were hung around his neck and he were drowned in the depth of the sea" (Matthew 18:6, NKJV). It is that serious, and that is the reason that I am sounding the alarm from the beginning. If you are not born again, you are not qualified to teach in children's Sunday school. It is for your good. You have two options: give your life to the Lord Jesus Christ or otherwise quit the ministry fast!

Are you filled with the Holy Spirit?

Working with children for several years, I have come to realize that we are on the frontline of a battle with the kingdom of darkness over the souls of these children. While the devil will be so happy with us if all we do in children's church is play soccer, go camping, hunt for Easter eggs, and have Santa Claus give out gifts during Christmas, he will certainly attack whenever we know and exercise our rights and authority. He will attack whenever we intentionally go out of our way to lead the children to Christ. He will not be happy with us if we are breaking the bread of life for the children and teaching them to rightly divide the word of truth. Unfortunately, we see many teachers who go with the flow and sleep on their night watches. To simply set aside times to seek the face of the Lord and bring the children before His throne of mercy is a chore. This is where we need the Holy Spirit. It may not be a requirement to teach in the children's church, but certainly, it is a necessity to be baptized in the Holy Spirit and start manifesting the gifts of the Holy Spirit. Every teacher needs to be baptized in the Holy Spirit. We all need to ask the Lord for the gift of discerning of spirits, among other gifts. There have been occasions when I entered the class with great lesson plans and, trying with all my might, made no headway. I would feel as if I was throwing a ball against a solid concrete wall. Nothing I did got to the children. During those times, managing the class was nearly impossible. On many such occasions, I discerned that I was contending with principalities and powers for the attention of the children. I would then address the spirits instead of yelling at the pupils or sending them to a timeout. We got dramatic results. The class would quiet down, and the children followed my instructions.

There is nothing as gratifying as seeing your pupils worship and manifest the gifts of the Holy Spirit. After the children in our class received the baptism in the Holy Spirit, we saw them manifest different gifts. Some prophesied, and their prophecies were right on the mark. Once, some of the teenagers who had graduated from our Sunday school went to minister in a national Christian concert called Livingspring, under the aegis of a youth group that they started called the Beacons. This was after we had a great Pentecostal experience. We knew that they were not going out to entertain but to minister to the people. After the ministration, they retired to our Sunday school hall to thank the Lord. We joined them. We all held hands and formed a circle. As we started to sing, "Bind us together, Lord, bind us together with chords that cannot be broken, bind us together, Lord, bind us together Lord, bind us, together in love," something supernatural

47

happened. The only way I can describe it is this: It was like a stream of electric current passed through all of us. It was a sweet shock that, rather than jolt us, seemed to unite all of us. We all still held hands as the current passed from one person to the other. When the young people realized what happened, they were ecstatic. They kept asking one another, "Did you feel the electricity?" I believe that the Holy Spirit visited us at that moment with a special anointing. Most of the children in the group that night have gone on to become great ministers of the gospel of our Lord Jesus Christ, either as pastors, worship leaders, gospel artists, or in other ministerial positions.

I will discuss the Holy Spirit's work in our lives as children's teachers more in detail later, but if you have not received the baptism of the Holy Spirit with the evidence of speaking in tongues, this is the time to earnestly desire it. If you have received the baptism, do not be content with just speaking in tongues, desire to manifest the gifts of the Spirit. Once equipped, seek to minister the baptism to the children. That is the way to get tangible results in the ministry.

Do you love the children?

The answer seems obvious, but I still need to ask this question. Do you love the children that you teach? Every teacher will tell you how much they love children. That is the reason they signed up to teach in the children's church in the first place. Well, that is not the total picture. I have met teachers who confessed to me that they joined the children's department because there was a need and there were few hands available to help. Others told me that they were obeying their pastor. Someone told me that she felt that her calling was to sing in the choir, but her pastor asked her to go to the children's ministry, and she obeyed. There is even a modern "scientific" approach that some pastors and ministry leaders use to determine spiritual gifts and ministries. If you desire to be a worker in the church, you take a survey and score yourself, and by aggregating your scores, you come up with some numbers which are supposed to be predictive of your spiritual gift. It is a psychometric analytical method like the instrument that psychologists use to predict behavior. Unfortunately, this has great potential for misleading and catastrophic outcomes. The analysis is as good as the information or data fed into it. However, what do you do when your pastor can bet her life on the accuracy of the analysis in determining your spiritual gifts? I must confess that it is scary if we are now using science to tell people what gifts of the Holy Spirit they have. This, to me, is like saying that spiritual things are scientifically discerned. I am a scientist, but I will not try to meddle with some things. What do you do when your pastor tells you that your spiritual gift is that of a teacher after you had taken the survey? I will be more comfortable if the pastor can hear directly from the Holy

Spirit and tell me or encourage me to hear from the Lord directly, rather than engage in a ten-minute quick fix in his office. That is how some people have ended up in the children's ministry without the anointing to teach children. The anointing makes the difference. It creates an infinite love for them. The consuming desire to have them on the right path which does not diminish over time. Loving the children that you teach even when they are at their worst behavior is not easy. You need the help of the Holy Spirit. If you are doing the work as a duty and not a calling, you are likely to burn out so fast. You may want to take a break, go to the Lord in prayer and ask Him for the anointing to carry on with the work. It is no use struggling in ministry. Find out from the Lord what your correct lane is. You will be more effective if you do.

Do you hear from the Lord?

Asher is one of the children in my class currently (in York, Pennsylvania) who asks me questions that seem far beyond what I expect from a child his age. After church service one Sunday, he stayed back in class to ask me a burning question. He was determined to get an answer. His mother was hurrying home, but when she came to my class to pick him up and saw that Asher was engaged in a serious conversation with me, she waited in an adjoining classroom. Asher said to me, "Dr. Innocent, could you please tell me how you hear from God?" Can you imagine what trouble that I would have been in if I did not know how to hear from the Lord or if I never heard from the Lord? A child sees his Sunday school teacher as the epitome of spirituality, and that is what we should be to them. I spent the next twenty to thirty minutes sharing my personal experiences hearing the voice of the Lord. He pelted me with questions, and I explained a few scriptures to him. Thank God for his mother, who understood what that conversation meant to the boy. She waited patiently and did not interrupt our discussion. Although she did not know the subject of our conversation at the time, she told me later that when she saw Asher having the conversation with me, she felt that it was something very important to him. I do not know how much impact that conversation had on the boy's spiritual journey, but I believe that sharing my personal testimonies gave him a lot of confidence in me. The same boy said to the entire class sometime this year just before we went on lockdown because of the COVID-19 pandemic, "Anytime that I am around Dr. Innocent, I feel safe." I believe this was his own way of saying that he felt confident or spiritually reassured around me. Does that feeling of safety have anything to do with the conversation we had? I may never know.

When I was teaching in the College of Medicine of the University of Port-Harcourt in Nigeria, my wife and I taught

51

two different classes in Our Savior's Chapel children's Sunday school. One Sunday morning, we got to the church and were told that our children's Sunday school superintendent and her deputy traveled and requested that we take care of the children's church. Hitherto, our children's Sunday school was very structured. We had set times to pray, teach the approved lessons for the day, go back to the general assembly, get the final instructions, and dismiss the children for the day. It was a very efficient routine. I wanted very badly to introduce the children to an extended worship experience but felt that we should abide by the structure that we met when we joined the children's Sunday school about six months or so earlier until the Lord opened that door. This Sunday, the Lord gave me the opportunity that I had waited for since we joined the church. I felt a nudge in my spirit to take the children through the kind of worship experience the children we taught at our previous chapel had gotten accustomed to. I seized the opportunity and told the children that we were going to touch heaven that morning.

As I led them in this new worship experience, the Lord spoke to my wife to leave her class and join me. She obeyed and came over. We continued to minister to the children together. At a point, she said that the Lord wanted her to pray for the children who needed the baptism of the Holy Spirit. A few children answered the call. Suddenly, there was a supernatural visitation. As she lifted her hand to pray for the children who came out, they fell down under the anointing. After a few minutes of praying, she decided to take the children to a different classroom to continue the prayer. However, one of the children, Biodun, got up, staggered, and fell down again under the anointing. She lay there on the floor for quite a while, evidently slain in the spirit. We continued the worship until Vickie was done praying for the other children who followed her to the next classroom. Biodun came around eventually and shared a beautiful testimony of how she met the Lord Jesus Christ while she was slain in the spirit. She described the experience where she was walking with the Lord along the bank of a river that was sparkling with beauty. The news of what happened that day spread. By divine orchestration, both our superintendent and her deputy had reasons again to be away from the church the following Sunday and once again handed the children's Sunday school over to us. We had another worship time and another divine visitation. Our superintendent got the report of all that happened in her absence and was so pleased. From then on, we had a lot more leeway in the way we conducted our classes as the Lord led us, and we had more and more experiences with the Lord visiting the children in very tangible ways. Sunday school was no longer a babysitting crèche for us but also a transformational garden where we planted the word of the Lord fresh from His throne room into the hearts and lives of these children. Those children have gone on to become responsible professionals and ministers of the gospel, serving the Lord in different ministries.

Candace Carr is a beautiful child of God with a heart of gold. She loves the Lord and loves working with young people. She is African American but feels called to work with the immigrant communities in the United States. We met her in our church in Chesapeake, Virginia, where she oversaw the youth church while I was the coordinator of the children's department. Candace was the guest teacher during the recent virtual hangout with my current Sunday school class. As soon as the state of Pennsylvania ordered a lockdown because of the COVID-19 pandemic, we met with all the teachers in our KidsZone (our children's department) and mapped out strategies to reach out to our children. Within a week, we created a virtual program that enabled the children to safely interact for two hours every Saturday using Zoom, an online meeting application. We called it Faith Class Hangout. It occurred to me that we could leverage the opportunity offered by this virtual environment and the lockdown to invite teachers and our former students from out of state to hang out with the children in our class. We hosted guest speakers from Florida, Virginia, Ohio, Pennsylvania, Indiana, Nigeria, New Mexico, France, London, Texas, and Maryland to hang out with our class. Nosa, a seventeen-year-old former pupil of my Sunday school class in Chesapeake and now a student at Harvard University, Sam, a sophomore at Yale University, and Seyi, a doctoral candidate in Stanford University and a gifted opera singer, all shared stories of their academic and faith experiences with the children. Mezie, a graduate of video animation, described the processes involved in creating 2D video animations while Gbenga, a broadcast engineer, walked them through what it takes to produce television programs. Dr. Grace Olugbodi, a math guru, Guinness Book of world records record holder, and the inventor of the math game *Race to Infinity* and our former pupil, spoke to them from London and shared her faith and experiences with math. She also shared the scriptures with them. Dr. Wande, Dr. George, Dr. Stella, and Dr. Kemi, seasoned Sunday school teachers, taught them and shared great insights from the scriptures with them. Candace, a youth leader and creative artist, shared the scriptures with the children and talked to them about photography. Chichi, a lawyer, a Florida supreme court certified mediator, and our former Sunday school pupil, also sang and played the piano for the children. Our children have milked the opportunity and asked the presenters all manner of questions, but the intense interest they showed when Candace mentioned her spiritual gift as the interpretation of tongues took the conversation to a different level. Candace was teaching them on the gifts of the Holy Spirit. When she illustrated the gift of tongues and the interpretation of tongues from her personal experience, the children wanted to know more. She explained how someone would be speaking in tongues, and she would hear the Lord whisper the interpretation into her ears, and she would interpret the tongues in a human language. From the questions the children asked, it was obvious that they wanted to know more, and I promised them that Candace would be more frequent on our guest speaker list.

I gave the examples above to emphasize the point that when you hear from the Lord and communicate with the children, you are far more effective than when you use all the psychology and teaching methods that you have learned. Let me ask the question again. Do you hear from the Lord?

Do you have a vision?

What is your purpose for teaching children? Do you have a clear vision of why you are teaching or would love to teach them? Can you articulate your vision for the children's ministry in a few sentences? If you have never thought about this question, do not feel terrible. You are in good company. I believe that more than 50 percent of children's teachers have never given it a thought. As teachers in children's ministries, we are leaders. Each of us has a "flock" that depends on us for guidance and direction. The responsibility to find green pastures for our sheep falls squarely on our shoulders. Having a vision of what to feed our lambs, where we are taking them, and when to feed them is fundamental to our effectiveness. Most of us simply follow a curriculum we got from the internet or bought from the bookstore. Others do not even use any curriculum. We are leaders. As leaders, we ought to be visionaries. Leaders look at the long-term outcome of their actions and project what the short-term approaches should be. Are you working with a long-term goal in view? If you have not given it a thought, you are probably like me during the early days of my ministry to children. When I started teaching children, I did not sit down and think through what the long-term outcome would be. I just knew that the Lord called me to the children's ministry in my local Anglican church, where the church leadership did not seem to give much consideration to who was taking care of the children and what they were being taught. It was a perfect environment for me to respond to the call. Born-again Christians in the country of my birth at that time were disparaged by the mainstream Anglican and Catholic churches as fanatics. The Scripture Union (SU) was at the forefront of Evangelical /Pentecostal Christianity in Nigeria in the seventies. The acronym SU was pejoratively used to brand born-again Christians of every stripe as the fanatics and never-do-wells of the society. To allow us to teach children in the church was indicative of how low on the priority scale of the church that the children's ministry was. They did not mind allowing us to babysit so that crying babies would not interrupt their liturgies. We found that a great opportunity to sow the seeds which the Lord watered, and by the late eighties and nineties, the products of our behind-the-scenes evangelical work took the Anglican church by storm. Most

Anglican churches in Nigeria today are not just Evangelical; they are Pentecostal. Much as the outcome of our children's ministry work was the explosion of Pentecostal Christianity in Nigeria, I did not have that long game in view.

However, the situation was different, starting from the late seventies and early eighties. We were intentional. We worked towards raising an army of young people who would become committed Christians all their lives. In the past twelve years, my personal vision has changed a bit. I have focused attention on empowering teachers and developing a model that children's ministry teachers can adapt to their training methods to effectively communicate the gospel to the children. I am keenly aware that no matter what methods we adopt, if the Holy Spirit is not given His rightful place in our teaching efforts, we are laboring in vain. That is why our teaching model emphasizes the Holy Spirit all the way. In Proverbs 29 verse 18, the Bible says, "Where there is no vision, the people perish" (KJV). May I suggest that you prayerfully consider your raison d'être for becoming a teacher in the children's ministry? The call is a marathon. It is not a sprint. If you must go the long haul, you must have a vision for the ministry. Write it down and follow it.

3

Who Are the Children?

If you know them, you will feed them appropriately

In the United States, every individual under eighteen years of age is regarded as a child. However, in most churches, we consider children to be non-adults who are under thirteen years of age. Most churches in the United States have separate classes for teenagers (thirteen to eighteen). In Nigeria, children under sixteen years of age are allowed in the children's Sunday school. For this book, however, I will restrict discussions to children under thirteen years old.

Since most churches make provisions for babies and toddlers, we shall include them in our discussions. For our purpose, we shall consider the following groupings:

Baby: 0-12 months

Toddler: 1-3 years

Preschool: 3-5 years

Grade school (junior): 5-8 years

Grade school (senior): 8-13 years

These classifications will help us understand the psychology and developmental characteristics of the children.

Babies

These precious, little, and adorable angels are the hope of the future. Their presence in a home is the ultimate definition of beauty. Having them in our children's church is always a thing of joy. However, they need special care. Children's churches should consider setting up special rooms (nurseries) and appropriate furniture for babies and their mothers. A section of the room can be partitioned for mothers to breast-feed in privacy. I do not encourage mothers to leave their babies entirely in the care of teachers. To provide for the spiritual nourishment of the mother, churches should consider—where practical—to stream their services live via You-Tube Live, FaceTime Live, Zoom, or any other technological platforms that will encourage the participation of the nursing mothers in the worship service in a virtual space, while taking care of their babies. Alternatively, television monitors with a direct feed from the sanctuary can be set up in the nursery. A teacher should be available to assist the mothers with any need. Teachers should also keep keen eyes on the toddlers and older children to make sure that they do not stray into the babies' room unsupervised. Preschoolers like playing "mom" and, if left with babies, would like to nurture and take care of them. They can easily feed the babies with some bright crayons, beads, shining nickels, or dimes and cause medical emergencies. (My daughter is a pediatric anesthesiologist. She told me that one of the cases she handled in her practice was a four-month-old baby whose big sister fed with quarters.) The bigger children in grade school like to carry babies. However, parents should not be encouraged to leave their babies with a seven-to twelve-year-old child. Much as they love the babies, my personal observation is that they get easily distracted and can drop the baby on the floor in a heartbeat, the same way they would abandon a toy to go for candy.

It would be useful to play soft background Christian music in the babies' room. There is something about music and children that I am yet to fully understand. I am aware of several scientific studies that report that early exposure of infants to music stimulates the development of the brain, helps in the regulation of emotions, promotes language development, sensory awareness, motor control, and social development, but it appears to me that there is more to music than what we already know. When we were expecting our first child, I made it a point of duty to sing for her as frequently as I could. When she was born, I continued singing for her every night, usually between 8 p.m. and 9 p.m. I did it for several weeks. One day I traveled out of town and would not be back until three days later. My wife reported when I came back that the baby cried so much the first night and would not stop no matter what she did to calm her down. Then she remembered that it was "singing time." The moment she started singing for her, the baby returned the favor. Both mother and daughter had a peaceful night. Babies' rooms in our children's churches should be equipped to play soft Christian music for the babies. People think of soft music as classical music. That is not what I am talking about. Classical music is soothing and recommended, but any music an adult can enjoy is good enough for the baby if it is not loud and jarring music with heavy drums and screaming noise. You do not want to overstimulate the developing brain. Gentle music will keep the babies calm and help their development.

Teachers assigned to the nursery should set out specific times to pray for the babies. It is challenging to pray for a person who is not able to say amen to your prayers. However, we should remember that the prayer of faith is potent. You are pouring your good wishes into the life of the child. You are decreeing blessings that may take years, if not decades, to manifest. Keep a prayer diary if possible, and it will surprise you in years to come to see the answers to your prayers. There is an insect called *periodical cicada,* which we do not see often. The last time we saw them was in 2004, but they are not extinct. During their season, they come out in their millions and announce their presence with fanfare. They make such synchronized buzzing sounds that one cannot help but notice that the *cicadas* are in town. What happens to them during the years of silence? The simple answer is that they are developing. They spend thirteen or seventeen years underground as nymphs maturing, and in *the fullness of time*, the adult insects emerge. They buzz around for about six weeks and disappear again for another seventeen years. A baby born in the year that periodical cicadas emerge will be a full-grown teenager when the next group emerges. Answers to the prayers you pray for a baby may not be apparent until her teenage years and beyond. The cicadas are not extinct; your prayer is not dead. Pray for the babies and wait for the manifestation of the answers in *the fullness of time*. All it takes is faith and patience.

Toddlers

They are putting out their first steps towards independence. At first, it is shaky, and they need a lot of help. With time, they become sure-footed and can stand on their own, then start walking and running. Before their third birthday, the toddlers have developed good locomotor functions and have developed enough vocabulary to express their personalities and needs, *albeit* in few words and short sentences. Generally, they are selfish. They do not like to share and often respond to many requests with "no." They also test the limits of your authority. Getting active and exploring the world comes with safety issues. Toddlers are prone to accidents. That is why it is imperative that any toddlers' class in our children's Sunday schools must have at least two teachers at any given time. Sharps, scissors, and sharpened pencils must be put away from their reach. So also, must beads, dimes, and nickels. Often when they pick up an object, it goes straight into the mouth. To help their cognitive development, we need to engage them in activities where they explore things. Simple puzzles and shape-sorting help their development. Learning blocks can engage them to no end. Allow them to dismantle and fix the blocks. Applaud them when they get it right. *Read* Bible stories to them. Teachers must prepare a variety of games well in advance to engage them fully. The American Academy of Pediatrics recommends that toddlers less than eighteen months old should not be exposed to so much screen time. They like to move around. Keep them moving without breaking things or fighting.

Toddlers love songs. Play simple songs for them and sing along. Also, encourage them to sing along. Do not sing complex songs for them. Songs that can be repeated as often as possible are the best. For example:

I am a child

Jesus loves me

I am a child

Jesus loves me

I would also recommend action songs like:

My head

My shoulder

My knees

My toes (repeat two times from the beginning)

They all belong

To Jesus

Wherever it is not possible to put them in a separate classroom, the toddlers can stay in the same room with the babies if there are at least two teachers at any given time in the classroom strictly monitoring and supervising their activities. Nursing mothers should not substitute for teachers. Much as their presence in the classroom provides extra eyes to monitor the children, we should remember that their primary reason for being in the nursery is to take care of their own babies and not another child.

Toddlers are beginning to learn the language to communicate with the world that they are born into. Let us, therefore, saturate their native language with the language of prayer. There is no better time to plant the culture and language of prayer into a child than when he is a toddler. Have you heard toddlers saying "I'll beat you" as part of the first phrases they learn in life? That is because the adult close to them uses that language of violence repeatedly. I chuckled to learn that my granddaughter was calling her mother "Babe." I am sure that you know the source of that vocabulary. She was keenly listening to her father. Have you seen the videos of toddlers "casting out the devil" or "praying in tongues"? They learned to pray like that from the adults in their lives. Teachers taking care of toddlers should model healthy prayer habits for them. Let them know that prayer times are special times that need their full attention. Make it a time that you get down on your knees and close your eyes while they are watching you. Tell them to do the same. Initially, they would treat it as another game. With repeated practice, they would get to know that prayer time is not a time for playing. Pray out loud and ask them to repeat the prayers after you. Snacks time is also a great time to teach them how to pray. Train them to pray *before* eating any food. That is the example that the Lord Jesus Christ gave to us. The scriptures say that whenever he had the opportunity to eat, he gave thanks. Beyond praying *with* the children, it is critically important that you also pray *for* them to their hearing. Watching you pray (as certainly they would) helps them develop the practice of praying. Knowing that you are praying for them and not yourself teaches them that prayer should not be selfish. They would learn early in life to consider the good of other people because you modeled selfless prayers to them. We would not know the exact age that they become spiritually aware. However, I believe that it is never too early to introduce the gospel to them. You do not know where they are on the spiritual highway. If we realize that it is the Holy Spirit who does the conversion, we should not hesitate to present the gospel to them. *The wordless book* is perhaps the best tool you can use to lead children that young to the Lord. Give it a try.

Preschoolers

Busy bees is an apt description of these preschoolers that we take care of in our children's Sunday schools. They are growing fast and rapidly developing physically, emotionally, intellectually, and spiritually. They are also establishing certain levels of independence. Running and climbing are com-

67

mon in this age group, especially the five-year-olds amongst them. They are voracious learners at this stage. This is the time to start introducing them to the gospel in a more intentional way. They are conscious of their spirituality and ask questions like, "If I do bad things, will I go to heaven?" I would suggest that as you tell them the story of Moses or Shadrack, Meshach, and Abednego, do not lose sight of their need for a savior. Use this opportunity to offer them the option to be saved. Lead them to Christ and do not doubt the authenticity of their confession of faith in Christ. Our first daughter received the Lord Jesus Christ into her life at the age of five. Later, when she was asked to give her life to the Lord again, she protested. She asked why she was being asked to do it again when she had already done so earlier. We did not ask her again, and she has remained an active Christian from that time till today. She has children of her own now. This emphasizes the need to present the gospel to the children as early as possible.

Grade schoolers (Junior)

On its website, The United States Center for Disease Control describes this age group as middle childhood.[3] The children are growing rapidly and developing more independence from their parents. They would rather play with friends than follow their parents when it is time to go home from church. They enjoy more outdoor activities that may involve a lot of running around and playing and would like to turn every activity into a game. The rapid physical, emotional, social, and spiritual developments noticeable in the preschoolers as described above are more intense in this age group. Intellectually, they are beginning to ask questions that you may not expect from them, although they still love to hear stories. In designing your curriculum, this is the age that most of the Bible stories will serve you well. They cannot have enough of the stories. They enjoy competition. They also enjoy recognition but would not mind if another child gets the prize. Teamwork is their greatest strength. When a natural leader emerges in their ranks, others simply follow him. The children in this age group quarrel easily and make up. Because they care much about their friendships, any misunderstanding among them does not last. They want to help, and teachers should engage them with age-appropriate tasks. Often, they seek their friend or teacher's approval. Compliment them when they achieve any goals or answer your questions correctly.

Spiritually, they are conscious of sin and are quite open to the scriptures. They may answer the call to receive the Lord Jesus Christ into their hearts as many times as altar calls are made. That is alright. Teachers should make sure that the salvation message is properly explained to them. Be clear in your choice of words. They respond well to the wordless

69

book. Encourage them to have personal quiet time with the Lord. From my experience, this age group is easily open to the Holy Spirit baptism. However, the teacher should take extra care in explaining the gifts of the Holy Spirit to them. Pray for wisdom and the Holy Spirit's direction as you handle this subject with them but do not hesitate to include it in their curriculum even if the curriculum you are using does not include it.

These grade-schoolers enjoy singing and can be trained to sing different parts and harmonize. They also enjoy reciting memory verses or poems. Our target usually is to have them memorize at least twenty verses of the scriptures in a year. Some of them can do a lot more. They like acting skits. However, they do better when the teacher comes up with the skits rather than ask them to compose one. Worship and singing seem to mean the same thing to them. The teacher is advised to explain the difference to them and take them through sessions of worship. When they understand what true worship is, they run with it.

Grade schoolers (Senior)

Children in this age group are highly active and are beginning to part ways with the world of fantasy in which they have lived hitherto. Consequently, they want true stories. Much as you can illustrate biblical facts and principles with

70

animal stories for younger children, this group needs the real stories. They are curious and want to know more. To illustrate some Bible lessons, I share testimonies of God's presence and interventions in my life and the lives of people that I know or have read about with them. In doing so, I make efforts to state the stories as accurately as possible. If there are gaps in my recollection of the sequence of events, I would use phrases like "I don't remember what happened next... but." When I am recounting a story that I read, I would preface it with something like, "I read the life history of..." That lends credence and authenticity to your narration of events. Children in this age group understand the concepts of sin and forgiveness. They are also conscious of fairness in dealing with each other and will also demand fairness from the teacher. Some pupils are adorable, while others are a real pain. It is easy to take to the pleasant ones and manage to endure the unpleasant ones. In the process, you develop favorites. It is natural. However, in dealing with children in this age group, I make efforts to treat them fairly, just like I did when I was raising my children. The truth is that the children who harass you today or give you great concerns may end up being your ministry arrowheads tomorrow. Let me illustrate this point with two examples from my experience working with this class.

Back in Nigeria in the late eighties, we had these children: five brothers and their only sister, and all of them were

71

at the same time in our Sunday school. These children were difficult to control. They would "stop over" at our Sunday school, and before we could take them to the classroom, they would disappear, and we would find them in the university's Natural History Museum or the nearby university zoo. It did not matter how many times we told the parents that the children they dropped off with us did not stay in class; they would repeat the same truant behavior at the next opportunity. My wife and I decided to make them our prayer project. With time, there was a dramatic change in their lives. Today, they are all very responsible professionals and ministers of the gospel. I know that one of them is a pastor and another one is a doctor who at one point was the coordinator of the Happiness Club when we left the university.

When I came to the United States, I had two sisters in my Sunday school class who tested my patience to the fullest limit. They would bring romantic novels and be reading them while in class and hardly followed instructions. For two years, my wife and I prayed for them and tried to make an inroad into their lives with the gospel. We would not give up on them. Before we left the church, the wall of resistance they built to shield themselves from the gospel cracked. They responded so dramatically to the Lord; the change was so radical that they burnt those novels on their own accord. Years later, one of them became the Sunday school teacher in the same class, where she gave us a lot of hassles. She is now a medical doctor, and her sister is a lawyer. Both are serving the Lord in different ministries. When you develop an interest in the pleasant children, do not forget that the others are watching. They know when you cross the line in your less than even-handed treatment of the difficult ones, and most times, they will call you out. As the ministers that we are, let us be humble enough to accept our mistakes and apologize to the children when we cross the line.

The children in this age group have an attention span of fifteen to twenty minutes. It is recommended that you plan your lessons and activities taking this fact into consideration. In my class, we plan four to five major activities every Sunday. We start with a prayer and worship session, followed by getting to know how their previous week went. Then the children are given about fifteen minutes to read the Scripture for the day and complete a comprehension exercise. We then do a word search game or crossword puzzle. Right after that, we present our lesson for the day and break the class into two or three groups to come up with a skit about the major lesson for the day. Before we close, we will have a prayer session. At times, one activity may be longer than twenty minutes, depending on how the Spirit of God moves in a meeting.

This age group likes to solve intellectual problems, and we must challenge them accordingly. Do not get frustrated when they pelt you with questions. They are learning to reason. Children in the earlier classes accept everything you tell them in faith and would hardly question you. It is not so with this class. They are developing fast and are getting exposed more and more to rigorous intellectual exercises in their schools and environments. We should help their critical thinking development by challenging them intellectually. If they ask you questions that you do not have good answers to, the honest thing to do is to let them know that you would research them and come up with answers. Do not shut them up to cover your lack of preparation. This is an inquisitive class, and you must be prepared for every meeting to answer questions ranging from why God created Satan to whether the big fish that swallowed Jonah was a shark or a whale or whether Jonah was dropped off at the continental shelf or on dry land. By the way, these are questions that I have been asked by my pupils. I did not just make them up. One way that I challenge them to think is to give them comprehension exercises with the last question asking them to freely give their insights into the passage they read. The amazing insights they give reveal the depth and range of their thought processes and spiritual maturity. Again, since they love memorization at this age level, I push them hard. In Chesapeake, Virginia, we had two children in my class who could recite more than one hundred memory verses. The two challenged each other to see who would get to one hundred and fifty verses first. They were at it before one of them moved to another state with her parents. Over here in York, Pennsylvania, we started a memory verse challenge about three months ago. As I write, two of the children, Sarah and Jaden, have each reached the seventy-five memory verses signpost. Olivia and Josiah have crossed fifty. The other members of the class are at different levels. Our goal is to have all of them memorize at least one hundred verses. From my experience, it is doable. At this stage of their development, their brains are like sponges. They can soak up whatever information that they are flooded with. A little inducement by giving them prizes or making it a competition creates the incentive that drives them further to achieve these goals.

Socially, the children are beginning to relate more along gender lines. The boys relate more with other boys, and girls create small "sisters'" groups, and each is protective of their gender affiliations. However, a few of them will start developing crushes for the opposite sex. Some years ago, I asked the children in my class what careers they would like to pursue when they grew up. Understandably, more than 90 percent of the class told me that they would like to be doctors, teachers, engineers, or lawyers. One girl gave me a rather curious answer. She said that she would like to be the wife of one of the boys in the class. That was her *career* goal. Evidently, she was having a crush on the boy and did not know how to handle it. My question provided her the perfect opportunity to make it public. It did not matter that her response had no direct bearing with what the question was designed to elicit. They are both college graduates now and have gone their different ways. As I write, she is not the wife of the young man she was hinging her "career" on. There is a possibility that her "career" ambition will be met in the future. I am keeping my fingers crossed. Teachers should be aware of this developmental milestone and know how to effectively manage their classrooms. Gossips and snitching are rife in this age group, and teachers should be prepared to be conflict arbitrators and mediators.

The hearts of children in this class are fertile grounds for sowing the Word of God. They recognize their need for salvation and are often willing to respond to an altar call. Just in case your pupils have not been offered the opportunity to receive Him as their Lord and personal savior, you should ensure that every child in your class is introduced to Christ. They also understand lessons about the Holy Spirit. We have seen them receive the baptism in the Holy Spirit with the evidence of speaking in tongues. If you have not taught your pupils about the Holy Spirit, you may wish to do so in your next lesson; otherwise, you may be depriving them of an experience that will change their lives for good and make your work as a Sunday school teacher a lot easier. You may need to do so over a couple of weeks. When my wife and I did it the first time, we taught the children over a period of six weeks. We even invited a guest speaker to give them his perspective on the subject. All the teaching prepared them for the conflagration that followed. It opened them up for receiving different gifts of the Holy Spirit. We saw the children go out to evangelize their peers without any adult prompting them to do so. They shared testimonies of the Lord speaking to them, and we had prophecies coming from some children during our worship sessions (I will share more about this in a later chapter).

While they are developing spiritually, they are also developing physically. The children have acquired a lot of talents that we can harness for the service of God. They can sing beautifully at this age and, if trained, can sing different parts to harmonize. They can play musical instruments and can be trained to preach. Any forward-looking Sunday school department will create an enabling environment to develop these talents. In our experience, within three years of introducing our Talents Development Program (see chapter 9), especially to this class, the children were ready to be used to serve the Lord in the church's choir or band. When they transition to the Youth class, they tend to be more engaged than if we did not develop their talents.

At this age, children have a deep love for God. In addition to leading them to Christ, I would suggest that you encourage them to develop a personal walk with the Lord. Teach them the value of having a personal quiet time. Ten minutes with God each day will transform the life of a child. Andy is one of the boys we taught many years ago. When he understood the concept of quiet time, he took it to a different level. He would take a personal walk at a given time of the day to be alone and have a conversation with God. The Lord visited him and gave him revelations which he shared with us and his parents.

This is an exciting class of children to work with. Unlike the younger classes, results of the teacher's work manifest in some cases, almost instantly and you can recalibrate your approach. It is also the senior class of most children's Sunday schools, where you have cohorts of children transitioning every year to the youth class. It is the capstone of their years as kids in the kids' church, and with it comes this feeling that they are "adults." That may explain some behavioral changes in some of the children. Also, there are visible physical changes that they go through during this period. Their growth rates are rapid. At times, these spurt growths may fool us to unconsciously think that some of them are "grown-ups." Some twelve-year-olds look like they are sixteen or seventeen, and we may be expecting more from them than other members of the class. Teachers in this class must do as much as possible to ensure that the children are grounded in committed Christianity.

4

The Digital Age

Interconnected communities: shared joys, shared sorrows

The digital age, also called the information age, is a historical period that started in the 1970s and was marked by an explosion of easy and rapid transfer of information worldwide, using the computer and other electronic devices. Although computing machines, later known as computers, had been developed as far back as the 19th century, they were not used for entertainment and social interactions as we use them today. Their primary usage was for crunching numbers. The first known computer was built in 1822 by the English mathematician Charles Babbage. Over a century of modifications and improvements of these calculating machines led to the development of computers which helped human beings to crunch numbers faster. For example, it was reported that as the United States population grew, it took about ten years to count and tally the results of its citizens during a census.[4] Computers shortened the time frame significantly. The early computers were large machines and occupied whole rooms. I remember that as an undergraduate student, our university had one computer room with this massive machine. The computer was operated by specially trained professionals. We gave them our data, and they fed them into the machine and sent us rolls and rolls of printouts.

Subsequent modifications of these massive engines led to smaller and faster computers. The invention of the much lighter personal computers and the internet gave rise to a technological revolution that would change the way human beings communicate, interact and conduct business all over the world. Speed used to be a major drawback in the use of computers. Growing needs for instant communication and information dissemination and retrieval created a demand for faster computers and the internet. Technological advances have made it possible to achieve both. The internet brought the world together and created what is commonly referred to as a global village. In some ways, the global village has advanced knowledge significantly and created relationships across geographical, demographic, religious, and cultural barriers. I remember that in 1982 when my fiancé (now my wife) was studying in France, it took about three weeks for my letters to get to her. If she replied to them the same day that she received the letters, it would take another three weeks for me to receive her reply in Nigeria. Since I had no telephone, the only means of communication was through letter writing. To communicate with her needed a minimum turnaround time of six weeks. We can achieve all that now in less than thirty seconds. That is the power of the digital age. We can now take photos of events here in North America, and in less than ten seconds, a friend in Tokyo, Japan, that we send the photos to is able to download and save them. Your entire classroom activities can be streamed live on Facebook, YouTube, or any of the social media platforms (I wonder what anyone reading this book ten years from now will think of these social media platforms. My hunch is that newer and better platforms and technologies will have emerged by then, and some of these current platforms will have become obsolete). People all over the world can be watching your class in real-time. That is the power of the digital age. Although the adoption of digital communication is nearly universal, it has a relatively young history. It will take us decades to fully understand its impact on the physical, emotional, and spiritual well-being of the consumers of these technologies. For now, there are some anecdotal observations and scientifically validated data that point to the advantages and disadvantages of the digital space that I think everyone in the children's ministry needs to take note of and be aware of as we try to help the children in our classes.

The internet is great

The internet is a huge resource where you can find information on literally any subject on the face of the earth. Type in any word in your browser and hit search. You will be amazed at the number of hits you will get. It is like you have a huge library in your palm or at your desk. You do not have to travel to Washington, DC to get access to the library of congress to research events that happened in AD 1600. Similarly, if you are planning a trip to the Museum of the Bible in Washington, DC, you would enjoy the trip better if you browse through the hundreds of artifacts you are likely to find in the museum by going to the museum's website. The internet becomes especially useful when you are preparing lessons for your class. For example, if you want to teach about laziness and you want to know what the Bible says about it, just google "Scriptures on laziness." Not only will the search engine turn up a listing of Bible verses that talk about laziness, but you will also see commentaries, blogs, and well-researched articles on laziness that will enrich your understanding of the subject. I do that quite often when I am preparing my lessons or messages. You will expand your horizon on a given subject by researching it on the internet.

Communication is a lot faster and cheaper on the internet. It is easier for those of us who lived before the internet became available globally to appreciate its value than those who were born in the digital age. We are no longer limited by distance. You can improve your knowledge on any subject by browsing and finding webinars that address your interest. Without stepping out of your home, you can attend a webinar holding in Australia or Ghana, or anywhere in the world. The later addition of video conferencing software platforms like Zoom, Adobe Connect, GoToMeeting, UberConference, Cisco WebEx, BlueJeans, Skype, Google Duo, etc., has created a new culture in communication. The video conferencing platforms provide the children's teacher resources that we did not have a couple of years ago. Like I said before, during this pandemic, I wanted to keep in touch with the children in my class and provide them a platform to interact with one another. We created a virtual hangout using Zoom. We met every Saturday evening for two hours. Initially, all we were doing was start the meeting and let them chat and play with one another in the virtual space. After two meetings, I discovered that the children loved it, and a parent asked me if we could increase the frequency. We were on lockdown, and the children were getting bored and lonely at home. I knew that the enthusiasm related to the chat format would wane once the novelty of the experience started to wear off. So, we came up with a variety of activities to constantly engage them, ranging from one of the children teaching her classmates sign language to some of them displaying their musical talents by playing musical instruments for the class from the comfort of their homes.

One variety that caught on and which opened my eyes to limitless teaching resources available to us was a program that we introduced in which we leveraged the power of the virtual world to involve teachers and mentors from out of state to share their life and Christian experiences with the children. We invited some of the pupils that we taught over twenty and thirty years ago to hang out with them. The first person we invited was Chinyere (also called Chi-Chi). She was one of the children we taught over thirty years ago in Nigeria. She is a lawyer and a Supreme Court of Florida certified Mediator. She is also a powerful singer and worship leader. Chi-Chi played the keyboard and sang for the children from her home in Florida more than 900 miles away. She then told them stories of her growing up years and career journey. She went on to field questions from the children on all kinds of subjects, including why she decided to study law and how long she had been singing. It was a hit. Next, we invited Nosa, a seventeen-year-old young man who was my Sunday school pupil in Chesapeake, Virginia, for eight years. Nosa is currently a student at Harvard University. He got tons of questions from the children on how he studied and what it took to gain admission to Harvard University.

We have had guest speakers from Ohio, Indiana, Harrisburg, New Mexico, Abuja in Nigeria, France, Maryland, London, etc., hang out with the children in real-time. They shared their Christian, career, and life experiences with the children. I also took the opportunity to ask some of them who have been longstanding Sunday school teachers to prepare Bible lessons for my class. Dr. Wande Oguntoyinbo taught them about missionary work, Candace Carr taught them about gifts of the Holy Spirit, while Dr. Grace Olugbodi taught them about conquering the giants. Dr. George Alao taught them about quiet time while Dr. Stella Onuoha taught them about loving their neighbors, and Dr. Kemi Ogusan, who used to be our Sunday school pupil many years ago, presented the salvation message to them. The children were so enthralled by the session with Grace, our former Sunday school pupil, who spoke to them about mathematics and 'conquering your giants" all the way from London. The major lesson I learned from the experience is that the issue of not having enough volunteer teachers for my class is now a thing of the past. I can schedule teachers from anywhere to teach my class virtually while I am on ground to manage the pupils. Since technology is native to the children, all I need is a television monitor and a laptop to get quality interactive instructions for my pupils. The caution, however, is for us to be sure of the teachers we are inviting to speak to the children and comply with all the applicable laws for such interactions.

YouTube has been derogatorily and sarcastically described as a "university" by some authors. If a university is an institution of higher learning where individuals acquire a specific body of knowledge to distinguish themselves in defined career paths, then YouTube is a *quasi*-university, in my opinion. The reason I say so is that it is a repository of knowledge, both fake and real. The knowledge is freely available, and every individual who has the boldness to teach whatever he *thinks* that he has the expertise to teach is welcome as a "professor" on YouTube. There is no vetting, no interviews, and no standards. There are tons of self-serving rubbish posted daily on this video platform, but there is also great and useful information out there. Everyone is left to his own judgment. There are tons of do-it-yourself videos on YouTube, many of which have enriched our knowledge base. Some time ago my car brakes developed a problem. My mechanic ran his diagnostic tests and came up with what the problem was. He gave me a print-out of his diagnosis and what it would cost to fix it. My eyes popped when I saw a bill of about one thousand three hundred dollars. When my twins saw it, they were angry. They watched a couple of YouTube videos and told me that they could fix it. I am not sure that they had changed a car tire before then, and to trust them with car brakes sounded suicidal to me. They pushed so hard

86

to convince me until I yielded. While giving them permission to try, I developed an alternative strategy. If they did not succeed, I would take it to another mechanic. It might cost me more, but the confidence and knowledge they would gain by either failing or succeeding was priceless to me. They spent about seventy-eight dollars on the spare parts and fixed the brakes. To be sure, I took the car to another mechanic and told him what my boys did and asked him to review their work. He did and certified their work as excellent. We used the car to travel hundreds of miles without any issue. YouTube can be an excellent resource for a Sunday school teacher. There are several videos that can enrich the classroom experience, and they are all at no cost to you. I use them and urge you to critically review them and see which ones are suitable for your class. Praise and worship songs are all available for you to use. Plan your lessons and decide when to engage the pupils in praise and worship using selected YouTube videos as backups. Good Christian movies like *War room, Conquering the giants, Pilgrim's Progress*, and *The Encounter* are all free on YouTube. You can enrich your class lessons with these resources from YouTube. You can also find games and some activities that will engage the children effectively and add variety to your class activities.

There are a lot of advantages to using the internet. I commented on a few of them to help the reader see value in using the internet. I do not know what new technological advances would change our communication and information-sharing culture. The children's teacher is strongly advised to be creative and adapt technology to his/her use in reaching out to the children and impacting their lives for good.

Beware of the Internet

Although there are several good reasons to use the internet, and we highly recommend the service to children's church teachers, there are notes of caution that we would like to sound here. While surfing the internet or using any of the video platforms that I described earlier, please bear in mind that all that glitters is not gold. There are several dubious people who intentionally create and post false or sub-standard information on the internet. Some do it for mischief, while others do it for money. In the latter case, people intentionally create viral videos and narratives which are patently false or half-truths. The wide circulation of their posts draws the attention of advertisers to their websites, and they can make some money off these half-truths. Others do it to create confusion in society. In recent times, some conspiracy theories have been circulating on the internet, linking the 5G network to the cause of the coronavirus pandemic.

While obtaining information from the internet, we are advised to do so circumspectly. We must do our due diligence because we own any information that we feed the children with. It does not matter what the primary source is. If in doubt, ask yourself these questions; "What will Jesus do with this information?" Or "What does the Bible say about this?" Do not allow your personal biases to trump an honest answer to these questions. One of our teachers, who has done very well during this pandemic communicating with children in her class and their parents, sent me a video that she planned to send to the children for review. The video is a good presentation of the Easter story, and I would have recommended it if I stopped reviewing it at the fifteen-minute mark. Somewhere after that, the presenters deviated from the central gospel message of the resurrection of our Lord Jesus Christ to talking about Easter eggs. That was a distraction from the gospel message, and I do not have tolerance for such distractions. I flagged the video and advised the teacher against sending it to the children and their parents. There are mistakes that you cannot afford to make once because they have eternal consequences.

Surfing the internet has the potential of wasting your time if you do not have personal rules on how to do it wisely. It will be a good idea if you give yourself a limit to how much time you can spend searching for a piece of information. If not, you can easily get lost in the maze of information out there on the web. You may start your search journey about the Holy Spirit and the gifts of the spirit. As you click on the subject, the search engine turns up both your primary subject of interest and related topics. If you are not disciplined about your search habits, you may keep clicking on related topics until you end up reading about Marilyn Monroe or NASA's *Voyager 2*. By the time you get off your desk, you would have blown through two hours of your precious time without getting a good grasp of your original interest in the Holy Spirit and gifts of the Holy Spirit. It requires discipline.

Addiction may be a strong word to use in describing the use of the internet by young people. However, internet addiction is becoming a clinical reality. Attempts are being made to define what could be regarded as internet addiction, but at the time of writing, there is no consensus on the subject. However, it has been largely described as the inability of an individual to control the use of the internet despite known adverse or negative consequences. Some scientific studies indicate that up to 25 percent of adolescent internet users display a pattern of use that could be described as pathological. The most problematic use of the internet by young people is in social media interactions and video games. A clinical diagnosis of gaming disorder is not defined in the current DSM-5 (Diagnostic and Statistical Manual of Mental Disorders; published by the American Psychiatric Association) but listed as one of the conditions that more research is warranted. As children's teachers, we are likely to be confronted with this issue as more and more pre-teens are getting more dependent on the internet as a normal way of life. We need to equip ourselves with information to detect, manage, and refer such problems when we observe them to parents and the appropriate agencies to get help for the children.

Many websites are demon-engineered to corrupt the children and sow seeds of immorality and violence in their lives. Part of being a responsible teacher is to identify the struggles the children are having, trying to resolve the conflicts of moral prescriptions of the scriptures and the negative influences of the websites that they visit. By planning a "town hall" meeting with your class, it is easy to identify what they are getting exposed to and help them navigate through them. This is how I do it in my class. I set aside a Sunday during which I do not teach anything. I tell the children that we are having a town hall meeting and ask them to sit down with their chairs in a circle or any other relaxed format. I would ask them to give me feedback on some of the lessons we had covered, and in that relaxed atmosphere, I would ask some probing questions and elicit the information that I need. Any hint of them going to websites that they should not, reading bad books, or watching movies they should not watch gives me an opening to explore more. The essence is not to shame or condemn them but to help them recognize the significance of their actions. In a group setting, they are usually forthcoming with such information. Oftentimes the other children in the class call them out for accessing some websites, reading certain literature, or watching some of the movies they watch. That serves as a deterrent. Occasionally, it gets into a debate if the children are not sure, and they would ask for my opinion. I would then go on and discuss the implications of accessing the websites and show them what the scripture says about such activities. If need be, I would talk with the child I identify that is accessing potentially dangerous websites on a one-on-one basis the same day before the close of Sunday school. If I think that the pupil needs further help, I will escalate the concern and let the parents know what is going on. Using the internet is like taking medicine. Despite its great potential for good, it could have some debilitating side effects. Watch out for the devastating side effects and avoid them.

Social Media and the children

There was a time when information in the electronic or print media was transmitted in a monologic form. In this format, the consumers of information were usually at the receiving end while the producers controlled what information the consumer received. For example, newspapers and radio stations decided the content of the information that they fed to the reading public and listening areas of their broadcast. Responsible media houses put great quality control measures to what was acceptable and what was not—a kind of self-censorship, in order to maintain their brand and protect their reputation. Communication was largely unidirectional. Comments on contents of broadcasts or articles in the newspapers were subjected to editorial reviews before publications. Much as that is still happening with the traditional media, a democratization of information dissemination through the internet has given rise to several dialogic media in which communication is bidirectional. The individual who originates the information gets unfiltered responses in real time.

Everyone who has access to the internet can create content and post on whatever platform that he chooses if he has the access. The reaction to the content from members of the public that have access to this post creates a two-way social interaction between the producer and recipient of the information. A community of people with common interests interacts and socializes in this virtual space, giving rise to several social media platforms that cater to general or specific interests. With technology getting cheaper by the day, more people have cell phones and internet connectivity, which makes texting, sharing personal pictures and videos, chatting, and socializing in the virtual space relatively easy. A new social media culture has evolved within the past decade, and the children that we take care of are growing in this virtual, occasionally unrealistic environment. Their characters and outlook on life are being shaped by the myriad of social media platforms literally at their fingertips.

I have observed that children (especially preteens and teenagers) tend to discover and adopt new social media apps faster, and as soon as the older generation begins to show interest in these apps, the children migrate to newer ones. There was a time Facebook was the rave for teenagers. When the baby boomers came to town on Facebook, the kids migrated to Twitter and quickly abandoned it and then off to Instagram and Snapchat. Most still have their tents pitched in Instagram and Snapchat, but others have flown away to TikTok, Discord, Kik Messenger, Live.me, YouNow, Whisper, Monkey, Yubo, Omegle, and many others that teachers and parents have no clue that they are using. Kids are interacting with complete strangers and living their fantasies online. Many of them are emotionally fragile and vulnerable to online predators and bullies who use the secrecy of the virtual environment to inflict emotional wounds and promote ungodly behavior amongst the children. We need to help them navigate the realities of the social media environment. Here are some suggestions that will help us understand and help them.

Educate yourself: By searching the internet, you can find several apps that are not commonly written or talked about. Children generally like to use the less known apps, especially if they are free. Most do not want their parents or any adults looking over their shoulders, and the more obscure the app is, the more attractive it is to them. Unfortunately, this element of secrecy is what gets them into trouble. Online predators practically hold them hostage when the children fall into their traps. I will encourage teachers to read blogs and articles that review the nature and activities that go on under the radar on these social media sites.

1. Get information from the children: By listening to the children while they are chatting during the "healthy noise" period, you will be able to pick up information about the social media apps that they use. I did not know about TikTok until I heard the children talk about what they were doing on that platform. You may also steer your conversation with the children during your "town hall" sessions towards different types of apps that they are using. In a group setting, they are likely to reveal which apps they and their friends are using.

2. Organize social media awareness campaigns: Set apart some time every year and organize seminars to educate and update teachers (and possibly parents) on issues about social media and the use of the internet by children. Including parents in the awareness program helps teachers mitigate potential risks and damages that the children may be exposed to. The campaign also helps the teachers to keep abreast with the recent technologies and activities on different so-

cial media platforms.

3. Plan reality check sessions: Plan to have sessions when you will have frank talks with the children concerning the advantages and harmful effects of the internet and social media on their physical and social development. It may be advisable to bring in experts who will work them through healthy uses of the internet.

Legal issues

Let me start off with a disclaimer. I am not a lawyer, and the opinions that I express here are my personal opinions, and the reader should please see them from that lens. Many churches, in my opinion, do not pay enough attention to the laws guiding certain practices among members of the church. Often, it is not because they do not want to but that they do not know what the legal requirements are or have the resources to ensure that they comply. Thankfully, there are free legal services provided by Christian lawyers to help ministries perform the assignment given to us by the Lord without any fear of running afoul of the law. This is particularly important when it comes to working with children, especially in the United States. Take, for example; there are eleven states, including Maryland, California, and Illinois, that require consent from the two parties to a conversation in order to make a telephone or in-person recording legal (you may wish to check up the current list by searching "two-party consent states" on the internet). In this era of ubiquitous cell phone recordings and transmissions across state lines, I will suggest that you get legal advice before you do any recordings with the children in your class. It may be a joyous moment for your class that you are recording, and you would want to share the joy with parents. Unfortunately, some people may not like their children to be recorded or even have them participate in a video platform chat. Do not let your good be evil spoken of. In a situation where you are not sure, I would advise that you send a parental consent form to all parents indicating that some of your activities may be recorded and possibly shared with other people. Have them sign the forms and return them to you for your files.

I will suggest that children's ministry leaders check with their churches or ministry policies regarding legal best practices for activities on the internet. If your church or ministry does not have them, please initiate a process to put the policies in place. All the teachers in the children's department of your church or ministry should be properly apprised of this information. Part of the onboarding process for new teachers should include these policies in your package for them.

5

Feed My Lambs

Growth results from a balanced diet

I joined the children's Sunday school class of a church we moved to. The teachers in the class were teaching a series on Christian apologetics. After about six weeks of watching them teach about Islam, Buddhism, new age religions, Confucianism, etc. I got worried. I was concerned that most of the ten to twelve-year-olds did not even know how to pray, and there they were being taught week after week about Mohammed, Buddha, etc. They were supposed to be trained to be the defenders of the faith when nobody had taught them about the Holy Spirit, and I was not sure how many of them were already born again. I complained to the pastor in charge of the children's ministry, and the situation was taken care of. Part of the reason the children in some churches go through the children's Sunday school system without being committed Christians is that the children's teachers either overfeed them with adult theology or underfeed them with permanent baby formula. We need to be intentional in creating the appropriate spiritual menu for our classes.

What do you feed them?

Teaching children can be challenging. Many ministries have done excellent jobs helping with curricula that are targeted at developing the children spiritually. That is great. Some others have concentrated their efforts on generating vacation programs. That is wonderful. I shall be discussing a different approach to children's ministry in a later chapter and share our experience applying different approaches with you. For now, let us take a closer look at the core issues that every children's ministry must concentrate on.

The salvation message

The starting point of our ministry is to ensure that every child that passes through our class has an opportunity to give his life to Christ. Think of it this way, if all the training that a coach gives an Olympic team is only for members of the team to remember at a future date that they were members of the national Olympic team, without the team ever partic-ipating in an Olympic event, all his efforts are worthless. If his team members do not participate in the Olympics, none will win a prize. If none of your Sunday school pupils makes it to heaven, you have wasted your time. There is a golden prize to be won - an eternity with the Lord in a city where the streets are made of gold. Only born-again believers qual-ify for the prize. Our primary calling, therefore, is to lead every child in our care to the Lord. The Child Evangelism Fellowship in the United States and Children Evangelism Ministry in Nigeria and some other ministries have devel-oped so many resources to help teachers realize this primary goal. However, the teacher's primary resource is the word of God—the Bible. Study it, understand it and teach. It is a good practice to study the Bible with a Study Bible, which has cross-references and a concordance. I have used Dake's annotated Bible for more than thirty-five years. Whatever else you teach the children, the salvation message should never be lacking in the menu. It is the primary food to feed them with.

Prayer

I have been shocked a couple of times that I asked an adult or a child to start a meeting or Sunday school class for us with a prayer. They froze and, in a few cases, started to hyperventilate. Over the years, I have discovered that you could gauge the spiritual environment that a child comes from when you ask him to pray. The child that comes from a home where an adult prays enthusiastically jumps into it and hits all the right notes effortlessly. On the other hand, a child who comes from a scattershot spiritual environment lumbers through a few sentences of prayer over what seems like an eternity of torture. Some pray prayers that one could consider irrelevant because they are totally off base. For example, you ask an eleven-year-old child to pray the opening prayer for a Sunday school class session, and you hear something like, "God, I hope you will help us to sleep well, bless our mummy and our sisters. Thank you for our food in Jesus' name." When I hear such prayers, I know that the child in question has not been taught how to pray. I suggest that the teacher fills the gap right away. Here is what I do. I tell all the children in my class that prayer is like having a conversation with God, just like they have conversations with their friends or parents. An easy way to remember how to proceed is to use the acrostic ACTS which I was taught in the Scripture Union Fellowship when I was in high school. A stands for adoration. C, for confession. T, for thanksgiving and S, for supplication.

Adoration: Tell the children to learn the names and attributes of God and start their prayers by calling him such names and using the attributes. For example, Lord God Almighty, the Ancient of Days, the Beginning and the End, Alpha and Omega, Jehovah, the Creator of the universe, God of peace, amazing God, El Shaddai, etc.

Confession: Some of the children may not know what to confess. You need to guide them. Tell them that confession is telling God any bad thing they did. Were they mean to another child? Were they disrespectful to their parents or teachers? Did they take what did not belong to them without permission from the owner? Having started on this track, the children will supply the other possible things they did wrong. I tell them to tell God something they did that God was not happy about and for which they are sorry. That is confession and repentance. I assure them that when they confess and repent, God will forgive them. The scriptures back me up on that (1 John 1:9).

Thanksgiving: Tell them to remember as many things as they can that they are thankful to God for, like good health, food, their parents, and homes, and tell God that they are grateful.

Supplication: Tell them that supplication means asking God for something, like God's protection, God's help for their schoolwork, praying for a friend who is sick, for safety whenever they are traveling on the road, etc.

In addition to using the ACTS format, I teach my pupils to be specific when they pray. You do not pray like "God, please bless the whole world." When he does, you may not know. Rather, pray something like, "God, I need a new pair of shoes; please provide my dad the money to buy me shoes by next week." If I ask them to pray for us to start a class, I am expecting to hear something like, "Lord, thank you for bringing us to church today, help each one of us to learn something new that will make our lives better in Jesus' name I pray. Amen." Being specific helps the child recognize answers to prayers. I remember an occasion that drove this point home for me several years ago. We had just ended a Sunday school session. The children lived on the campus of the school of nursing a few blocks from the chapel where we had our Sunday school. As we closed the meeting for the day, this huge storm rolled in with a heavy rain. Typically, this type of tropical rain would last about forty-five minutes to one hour. The children worried that they would not get home soon. They asked me how they could get home. Since it was a walking distance from where they lived, I did not expect their parents to come for them. I asked them to pray that the storm would stop within ten minutes, and they did. God answered their prayer swiftly. As soon as they finished praying, the heavy downpour stopped miraculously.

The sky cleared, and they were all able to walk back home. Their prayer was laser-focused. There was no time to beat about the bush. Each one could identify what happened as an answer to their prayer. That is the kind of experience that builds faith in the children. It was a supernatural experience that they would not forget in a hurry. We need to teach the children that prayer is the master key to unlocking the supernatural intervention of God in our daily lives. When they experience a supernatural event, the desire to pray more gets intensified.

The Holy Spirit

I would not like anyone reading this book to make the same mistake that I made in the early years of my ministering to children. From 1972 when the Lord called me to the children's ministry until 1985, I did not teach the children about the Holy Spirit. I think part of the reason was that I believed that the children were too young to understand who the Holy Spirit was, and the concept of baptism in the Holy Spirit and gifts of the Holy Spirit were too advanced for them to comprehend. I also felt that they would "misuse" the Holy Spirit. Again, I believe that part of the problem was that personally, I did not receive the baptism in the Holy Spirit with evidence of speaking in tongues until the late seventies. It was easier to sidestep the uncomfortable subject because I could not give what I did not have. However, that was a huge mistake.

105

Rather than avoid teaching the subject, what I should have done was confront my personal deficiency and truly seek the baptism of the Holy Spirit. To compound the issue, the curriculum we used in our Sunday school did not treat that subject. In retrospect, I believe that every children's Sunday school curriculum *must* include a comprehensive teaching on the Holy Spirit and the gifts of the Holy Spirit. For that reason, I will devote a chapter of this book to the subject.

Integrity

There are several scriptures that talk about integrity, honesty, doing right all the time, etc. We shall teach and model integrity as part of our Christian ethics to the children. We do not have to shy away from this important subject. It is important to the Lord. That is why it is emphasized in different ways in both the old and new testaments. The Lord says, "Be *you holy for I am* holy" (1 Peter 1:16). Paul wrote to the Philippian church, "Finally, brothers and sisters, whatever is true, whatever is noble, whatever is right, whatever is pure, whatever is lovely, whatever is admirable—if anything is excellent or praiseworthy—think about such things" (Philippians 4:8, NKJV).

It is good for our pupils to cultivate the culture of honesty while they are still young. It will serve them well when they grow up. In a world where telling lies is becoming a national pastime, men and women of integrity will stand out as beacons of hope. The best place to start inculcating that in a growing child is the children's Sunday school. We have the opportunity to teach the children to recognize sin for what it is and "flee every appearance" of it. I get concerned, especially here in the United States, when I see adults treat sin with kid's gloves in the name of being politically correct. No wonder the American prison population is the largest in the world. The children are not trained to detest sin while they are young. As they grow older, they see sin as a normal way of life until the law catches up with them and throws them into prisons. It appears that the system is designed to punish rather than correct these young people. Obviously, the adults in the lives of these young people fail them. Will the church also fail them? That is the question you and I, who have been entrusted with the responsibility of molding their characters, need to answer every Sunday that we have the opportunity to lay a building block towards the destiny of the child in our care.

Recently, our pastor asked Vickie and I to give a talk on marriage and family stability. While I was praying about it, the Lord gave me an unusual approach to handle the subject. I requested all our five adult children to evaluate our own marriage by describing for me what impact our marriage had on their lives (whether positive or negative). Knowing that they would be candid in their assessments, I felt a bit nervous and vulnerable after posting the request on our WhatsApp platform. I asked them to reply to me privately so that they would not influence one another's response. They were candid like I expected but mainly on the positive side. Our last born said, "Since you were both present and you both communicated well, I feel like that is *why I didn't do some of the wilder things I wanted to do as a kid.* I knew I'd never get away with them." There was a deterrence that happened in his life because two individuals he loved and respected took more than a casual interest in his life. That shaped his life for good. He recently graduated from Seton Hall University in New Jersey and loves serving the Lord in different capacities.

The first time I opened a Facebook account, I had an avalanche of "friend" requests, mainly from the children I had taught in Sunday school over many years. Many of them that I had not communicated with for over twenty to thirty years expressed joy at the virtual reunion. Most of them expressed how our ministry impacted their lives. Let me share with the reader one of such notes from a "boy" I taught in the early eighties. His name is Bayo Oyedeji. Bayo studied medicine and specialized in cardiology. He wrote me sometime in 2009 and said,

It is so nice to actually read from you. Thank

God for this internet technology. I would be rounding off my one-year sub-specialty cardiology fellowship training at the National Heart Center, Singapore, in about five weeks. Will return to my family (wife and two kids) in Nigeria just before the New Year. What can we say than to continue to thank the Lord for your family? For all the investment you put into us in Happiness Club and All Souls Chapel. *You can be sure that we are passing it on to our own children* (emphasis his). These years formed and molded us. It is only now that we realize it. *Even when we "want to go astray," it became impossible to deviate from the path of Christian upbringing.* (Emphasis mine) Looking back, I don't think that anyone could argue that we could have had it better.

When there is an adult that a child can look up to as a mentor, especially one that lives a consistent Christian life, the child ends up being responsible. As teachers, we should not only teach our pupils integrity as described in the scriptures but model it. Modeling integrity to the children does not stop at the Sunday school or church service. If the chil-

109

dren can observe your activities in the outside world, they have a better picture of who you are, and you cannot afford to let them down. I attended a church service with my brother when I paid him a visit many years ago. Since that was my first time visiting that church, I decided to see what their children's Sunday school looked like and how they taught the children (I do that often when I visit a new church). When I got to the children's department, there were well over forty noisy children but no teacher in the class. The adult service was well underway, but there was no adult taking care of the children. I asked the children about their teachers, and they assured me that they had a teacher and that he would come. After waiting for about fifteen minutes and still no teacher in sight, I decided to engage the children. I do not remember the subject of my impromptu lesson that day, but I think that I taught them a song or two in addition. About thirty minutes or so later, this tall and smiling young man in his late twenties sauntered in, grinning. What followed embarrassed me. As if on cue, all the children started to chant, "Uncle late comer, Uncle late comer." The young man kept smiling and did not seem bothered at all. It looked like he was used to it. He was their teacher. I turned over the class to him, and he proceeded to teach without apologizing to the children. I did not have the opportunity to visit that church again.

Uncle Patrick (not his real name) was the secretary general of our Sunday school in one of the churches that I attended years ago. He shared this story with us in one of our meetings: He was on his way home after a busy day at the Sunday school and had some of the Sunday school kids that he was giving a ride in his car. At the campus gate, he was stopped for a routine check by some security men. For whatever reason, a heated exchange ensued between him and the security men. He hurled words at them that he later regretted using, and the men responded in kind. Eventually, they let him go. On the way, one of the children said to him, "Uncle, are we supposed to use those words and speak like that?" At that instant, he felt little. He knew that he failed the Lord and did not model Christianity to those children. Integrity needs to be taught, but more importantly, we need to model it to the children.

Hard work pays

In the United States, Asian immigrants (mainly Chinese and Indians) are regarded as smart. There is another smart nationality group that most people are not aware of—Nigerian immigrants. According to the United States census data, foreign-born Africans in America are the most educated, with 43.8 percent of them compared to 42.5 percent Asian Americans and 28.9 percent of immigrants from Europe, Canada, and Russia having the first degree. A subset of these Africans, the foreign-born Nigerians in America, is ranked the most highly educated, with almost one-third of all Nigerian-Americans having graduate degrees. I have interacted with Indians and Chinese at professional levels, and of course, I know the Nigerians quite a bit. One common thread that I have observed in these groups is hard work. Hard work defines their success. They do not give up easily. I do not believe that they are genetically more endowed to be smarter than other groups, but culturally, they seem to be pushed, or they push themselves to achieve success against all odds. My wife was doing her PhD in French before she came to the United States. Faced with the reality of an extremely narrow spectrum of job options, she abandoned the PhD and enrolled in a nursing program from scratch. She got her associate degree in nursing (RN) in 2007, worked as a registered nurse for a couple of years, and enrolled in two master's degree programs. She obtained a master of science (MS) degree in nursing and a master of business administration (MBA). In total, she has three master's degrees. These open multiple job opportunities for her. It was tough when she was in school, though. A Nigerian friend of mine was a practicing doctor in Nigeria. When he came to the United States, he did a master's degree in public health (MPH) and later went back to medical school and started all over. Today he is a specialist in internal medicine. Five of the pastors affiliated with the first church that I attended in Maryland when I came to the United States, CAC Bethel Fellowship Church, have PhDs in different fields. The church membership is small, and about 90 percent Nigerians. The church that I attend currently is a small church of about 115 adults and children from about eleven African and Caribbean countries. About 70 percent of members of the leadership team of the church have a minimum of master's degree. Our senior pastor is an MD and specialist endocrinologist. His wife, who also is one of our pastors, has a PhD. On May 10, 2016, Nigerians made history in Howard University, School of Pharmacy in Washington, DC. Of the ninety-six doctor of pharmacy graduates, forty-six were Nigerians.

Most of these immigrants know that one way of creating a future for themselves and their children is to follow the academic route. They would take up odd jobs while working on their medical, pharmacy, engineering, or accounting degrees. Hard work pays. This is a principle that we drill into our biological children, and it is a principle that I will encourage you to incorporate into your Sunday school programs.

Do not forget that a Sunday school is a school that holds on Sundays. It is a school where you equip the pupils with the tools and knowledge that they need to navigate the future. Apart from teaching salvation, prayer, discipleship, Holy Ghost baptism, evangelism, and other scriptural imperatives, we create sessions and programs to focus the children on noble career options. Our children's ministry is a comprehensive package. I have formal and informal career talks with my pupils, during which I emphasize that anything short of the best is not good enough for them. I am their mentor and coach. To create a culture of working hard, I brand my goals or expectations in such a way that they will be etched in their consciousness. For example, I have "Operation Fervent Business (OFB)" talks with the children. They believe in me because they sense that I have a genuine interest in their success. They have often returned the favor by working hard and getting to the pinnacle of their careers whilst remaining committed to following and serving the Lord. I do not know what the exact number is now, but by my last count, about fifty of the children that passed through our Sunday school and Happiness Club programs are now medical doctors. Five have PhDs. There are several pharmacists, lawyers, architects, engineers, accountants, and other professionals. Several are ministers of the gospel, with some pastoring big churches all over the world. Hard work pays.

Worship

The psalmist writes, "Give unto the Lord, O you mighty ones, Give unto the Lord glory and strength. Give unto the Lord the glory due to His name, Worship the Lord in the beauty of holiness" (Psalm 29:1-2, NKJV).

Worship is the very essence of our being. We acknowledge that the Lord is worthy of all praise and adoration. It is an act of reverence, an acknowledgment of the almightiness of God, and a yielding of whoever or whatever we are to the supremacy of our Creator. This is a message that we need to burn into the mind of the children under our charge. Starting from the toddler classes right up to the seniors in our Sunday school, worship should not only be taught; it should be practiced every Sunday or mid-week meetings. The children should be taught to worship the Lord on their own, with their family, and corporately in church when we gather. The psalmist says,

> Make a joyful shout to the Lord, all you lands! Serve the Lord with gladness; Come before His presence with singing. Know that the Lord, He is God; It is He who has made us, and not we ourselves; We are His people and the sheep of His pasture. Enter into His gates with thanksgiving, And into His courts with praise. Be thankful to Him and bless His name. For the Lord is good; His mercy is everlasting, And His truth endures to all generations.

Psalm 100: 1-5 (NKJV)

The psalmist sees value when we make a joyful noise (shout) to the Lord. Who can do that better than children? They love noise, and if we can channel all that energy to not just noise but a joyful noise unto the Lord, the children will love it, and the Lord will be happy with them and with us. This psalm also encourages us to come into the presence of the Lord with singing. Worship can be done quietly, but the Lord enjoys our singing. Get your children involved in singing during your worship times. It is okay to play songs and worship videos, but please get the children to sing along. They are not to be spectators. They are not to watch worship as a movie. Get them to participate. Personally, I prefer to teach the children the songs and let them worship the Lord singing the correct lyrics. That is what makes the difference in worship. As they sing, the words are translated into offerings and sacrifices of praise to the Lord. It is then that His glory comes down. Worship times are times when we call the attention of heaven to our spiritual environment. I imagine the Lord listening to our hearts of worship and asking His angels to minister to us. In our experience, times of worship have been times of manifestation of the supernatural experiences for our children. It is like the purity of the worship that comes out of the mouth of the children invites the presence of the Holy Spirit to our meetings. I remember when we produced our first album in 1986. It was our first experience, and the recording studio in Lagos, Nigeria, had not been upgraded for digital recording. That meant that once the red lights

116

were on, the singing must be flawless. There was no room for mistakes. The children must get it right, or we would re-take the song from the beginning. It was tough. There were songs that we would take to the end and before the red lights were off, one of the children would cough or say something that would compromise the recording, and we would start all over. We finished the recording around midnight. Relieved that they had achieved their dream, the children burst into worship right there in the studio with some secular profes-sional artists and the recording engineers watching. As the worship progressed, the Holy Spirit visited us and gave us messages through prophecies. Most of the times that we had the upper room experiences that I describe in this book were preceded by glorious worship times. Let us make worship in our children's ministries times of supernatural encounters, not just singing and feel-good times. These are indelible ex-periences that the children may not get elsewhere. This is the way they should go. When they grow up, they will not depart from it.

How do you feed the lambs?

I saw a picture circulating on the internet of a toddler who is probably less than twenty-four inches tall clutching a foot-long loaf of bread and drinking from an outsized cup. He looked pitiable. He had food in his hand, but the looks on his face were those of distress and one struggling to eat his meal. The bread was a burden to him even though it was meant to solve his immediate hunger problem. The issue is that the bread was not provided to him in a form that he could eat easily. He had food in his hand but was not able to eat it with joy. It was a chore. An adult could have done a better job of breaking the bread into smaller pieces for him. In a similar way, children in our care are surrounded by the gospel message, but how much of it are they consuming? This is where we need to get creative to make sure that our Sunday school children do not starve spiritually amid abundant spiritual food. As much as the food we feed them with is important, how we feed them determines how much spiritual nutrition they get.

Make it simple

While researching the charge that the Lord gave to Simon Peter in John 21:15-17 to take pastoral care of the believers, I ran into a fiery theological exchange by two individuals on the internet who are probably professors of theology or have some strong theological backgrounds. A non-English speaker (let us call him *Seeker*) needed help concerning this passage. Seeker said that he noticed that when the Lord gave Peter the charge, He first said, "Feed my *lambs*." Then, "Tend my *she*ep," and the third time, He said, "Feed my *sheep*." He said that the Bible in his native language did not differentiate between sheep and lamb. As he was reading that for the first time in the English Bible, he wondered if the two words were different. He checked on the internet and found that lambs were young sheep. He then went on to say that in his understanding, the lamb and sheep probably represented "new believers and advanced believers," respectively. He needed the help of English speakers to understand this scripture better. The first respondent to his request (let us call him *Wiseman*) agreed with Seeker's interpretation of this scripture and made the extra effort to give him the Greek root words for lamb and sheep as *amion* and *probaton,* respectively. Then someone (let us call him *Opposition*) challenged Wiseman's explanations by stating that he (Opposition) was not convinced of the answer as being correct because it left out multiple possibilities. To assert his superior knowledge, Wiseman said that he was following a "patristic hermeneutic" approach in his explanation of this scripture to Seeker, to which Opposition countered that there was no "infinite number of hermeneutical approaches." I was lost at this point, and I guess that the non-English speaker who needed help from English speakers to understand the simple difference between a lamb and a sheep in order to understand the eternal purpose of this command must have also been lost. That is the point. Preachers and speakers who like to display their egotistic superior intellectual endowments end up losing their audience. Children's teachers should find ways to break down biblical facts and doctrines to the children in a manner that is age-appropriate. Make it simple. The children

119

are still feeding on milk or semi-solid food. Use age-appropriate language and avoid theological cliches that make you sound intellectual but provide no nourishment for the souls of the young ones.

Give them precise instructions

Children need to be given clear and detailed instructions on not just *what* to do but *how* to do them. It is not sufficient to tell the children to pray. You will need to tell them what to pray about and how to go about it. For example, if you ask Junior to pray for the class at the close of the day, it is not sufficient to say, "Junior, could you please pray for us." An adult will understand what you mean, but Junior needs to be told that:

1. He should thank the Lord for the great lessons the class had.

2. He should thank the Lord for the teacher who taught the lesson.

3. He should commit the children into the hands of the Lord for safety as they go home and throughout the week and;

4. He should pray that God will bring everyone back to church safely the following week.

Junior is likely to repeat these lines but do not worry; he is learning to pray in the process. Use precise language in communicating with them. I remember once a little girl in our Happiness Club group came to us crying. She could not find her shoes, and it was time to go home. It was getting dark, and she could not find her shoes. All the teachers and the bigger children were mobilized to look for the missing shoes. Some precious minutes passed, and the search party was not making any headway. In exasperation, I turned to her and asked, "Where did you throw away your shoes?" The five-year-old turned to me and innocently replied, "Uncle, I did not throw them away; I lost them." The entire search party burst out laughing.

If you give them assignments, remember to specify when and how they should submit their responses. If you assume that everyone knows that when they complete their assignment, they ought to turn them in for grading, you may be in for a ride. Often you have a pupil that would finish the assignment and wait for the next instructions. When you are teaching them the word of God, be sure you know your story very well. Do not tell them that Judas Iscariot sold Jesus for thirty dollars or Jonah was in the belly of the whale for three days. Thirty dollars may be an easy way to help them understand the story but what the Bible talks about is thirty pieces of silver which do not amount to thirty dollars. Again, the Bible talks about the big fish that swallowed Jonah. It did not specify what type of fish it was. Some smart ones will fact-check you in real time by using their phones to check on the internet. All this comes to is that as a teacher, you need to be prepared before you teach the children. It does not matter how many times that you have taught the same topic before.

Teach them by examples

Do you remember the story of the young teacher that I told earlier who came late to his class and his pupils called him "Uncle Late Comer"? That was a bad example to present to the children. They are not just watching what you say; they are more interested in what you do. Our lives are supposed to model and reflect the gospel to them. If you habitually go late to events, express anger, or tell lies, the children will know. Do not take it for granted that they are young and will not understand what you are doing or saying. They will copy your actions and model their behavior on that template. You are reproducing your kind; it does not matter how much you pretend. Your actions may draw the children closer to or drive them further away from the kingdom of God. What you do or say outside of the classroom has even a greater impact on their lives, especially if they can watch from a close range. I was privileged to have all my five children pass through my Sunday school class at one time or the other. They also watched my behavior at home. I am glad that any opportunity that they have to talk about me gives me joy rather than palpitations. Commenting on her ideal marriage partner, one of my daughters said, "I keep telling people that your marriage is what makes me believe that marriages work and not all…men are unfaithful…Also, I have high standards when it comes to choosing a spouse because if they don't treat me the way you treat Momimo, I don't want it." Momimo is the nickname that our children call my wife. They call me Dadida. She was referring to the way that I treat my wife, Vickie. This is the highest validation of my work in the ministry. My daughter takes me as the gold standard when it comes to how a man should "treat" his wife. Unfortunately, many teachers do not have such testimonies in their homes and families.

Great teachers who have poor testimonies are not good role models for children and should find a better place to serve in the church that suits their temperaments and dispositions. In the children's ministry, your life is under the microscope and is constantly being scrutinized. We should model integrity, holiness, love, faith, kindness, wisdom, truth, spiritual insights, and righteousness to the children. We should also model hard work to the children. One of the reasons why I enrolled in a PhD program after obtaining a degree in pharmacy was to let the children that I had been encouraging to be the best they could be and get the best education they could get see that it was possible. I know that many of my students take me as their role model. It hurts me deeply when I find myself not measuring up to their expectations at any time.

Encouragement motivates hard work

We need the partnership of parents in this great responsibility that the Lord has given us. One way that I warm up to them is to identify at least one thing that their child is good at and call their attention to it. "Good day Ms. Anne. Are you Debbie's mother?" I would strike up a conversation with the parent. "Yes, I am." The default line is that most parents expect negative reports from teachers about their children. When I speak to a parent like this, they brace up for the negative report, and you will see it from their body language. I would then go on to shower the pupil with praises. "I am Dr. Innocent, Debbie's teacher. Debbie is one of the best singers in my class. With good coaching, she will go places." Now relaxed, the parent would proceed to volunteer more information about Debbie. "Oh, thank you, yes she sings like my mother. She spends hours in the shower singing. My only problem is that Debbie does not take her schoolwork seriously. Anyway, thanks for letting me know. I will enroll her in piano lessons." Every parent wants to hear that his/her child is a star. I can say that almost in 99 percent of instances when I took this approach, the parents responded positively and that opened the door for me to work with them to help the child become the best he/she could be. The other side of the coin is that the children also turn the corner when you praise them.

There is a primordial response to praise that brings out the best in every human being. Praise is a positive reinforcement. Animal trainers use positive reinforcement to train their pets. If you give a reward to a dog for a desired action she got right, she will learn that action faster than if there was no reward. The reason is that the dog will associate that action with a reward. There is also a negative reinforcement that you could use in training animals. If a particular action results in a punishment, the animal will learn to refrain from it, knowing the consequence. Similarly, encouragement motivates children to aspire to greater heights. Occasionally, punishments help. In my several years of teaching children, I prefer to apply positive reinforcements in bringing out the gem in the child. I like to give assignments in the class and reward the best three students in the assignment. Often, I would ask the children to stand up and have the entire class clap for them, or I would buy some inexpensive prizes for the children or use tokens to recognize their achievements or good behavior. Some may argue that only the smart ones will be encouraged to try. On the contrary, more than 80 percent of my class would try to get that prize the next time. To make sure that the prizes go round, I intentionally create prizes around the strengths of the children who may not qualify for certain categories no matter how hard they try because there are others who are far better than them in those areas. For example, if I find that there are only three or four children who take all the prizes for my comprehension exercises, I create other categories like "the best behaved," "the child that gave the best insights for the day," "the best actor," "the most punctual," "the most helpful," etc. Before the end of the year, my prizes would have gone round, and all the children have had a prize or a recognition at least once. Certainly, there are some that would dominate in many categories. As a follow-up to the prizes or recognitions, I would go to their parents after church service or when they come over to the children's Sunday school to pick up their child and let them know that their child won the prize for the day. Often, I would do that in the presence of the child.

Praising a child before his parents makes the child want to do more to impress both his parents and the teacher. My head teacher did a similar thing for me when I was in the third grade. He came to our home to tell my father that I was the best pupil in the class but added that I had one of the worst handwriting. My father was impressed to learn that I was the best pupil in the class and showered me with all the praises he could in the presence of our head teacher. You bet that I never took a second position after all that praise. I worked a little harder to maintain the first position in my class. How about the negative report on my bad handwriting? Again, my father did a wise thing. Rather than scold me for the bad handwriting in the presence of my teacher, he involved me in the discussion to find a solution to my problem. He asked me what I thought was the problem. At that instant, I had to come up with an excuse. I told my dad that it was the pen nib that I was using. He promised in the presence of my head teacher that he would buy me a new pen nib, and he did. He bought me the more expensive fountain pen nib rather than the regular one that all the pupils used. The ball was now in my court to prove that the excuse that I gave both gentlemen was the real reason for my terrible handwriting. Armed with my expensive fountain pen nib, I experimented with different kinds of handwriting. Luckily for me, my father had a beautiful cursive handwriting. I studied it and came up with a version that became authentically mine, which my classmates in high school and the university as well as my students, admired a lot. That one visit to our home by my head teacher changed the trajectory of my life in many ways.

To encourage the children in my Sunday school class to go for the best, we give big prizes for the more challenging tasks. For example, the first time I gave the children an assignment in my current church to memorize at least ten verses of the scriptures, only two pupils took the assignment seriously. I shocked the rest of the class by giving each one of them ten dollars. The following Sunday, some of the children came to class armed with ten memory verses. We clapped for them, but there was no ten dollars prize for their efforts. However, our memory verse challenge took off immediately like a rocket. Two years down the road, we are on another challenge. This time the target is one hundred memory verses, and the prizes are the dollar equivalent of the number of verses a child can recite. To qualify for a prize, a child must recite a minimum of fifty verses. I did a little fundraiser for the prize money. Our goal is to motivate the children to internalize the word of God and, borrowing a leaf from the national spelling bee competition, we decided to give cash this time, and it seems to be more effective than when we did a similar challenge in my former church and awarded trophies to the best pupils. In that church, the best student came up with about thirty-five verses. The second did about twenty-two, and the rest were under twenty verses. Within the same time frame, in the current challenge, two children have crossed the seventy-five memory verses checkpoint and are heading towards one hundred. Two others have crossed fifty, four are between forty and forty-nine, and the rest are between twenty-five and thirty-nine except for three who are yet to reach twenty. Positive reinforcement by rewarding excellence helps the children aspire to greater heights.

Discipline is necessary

Children come from different families with different standards and issues that they are dealing with, and, often-times, their behavior during Sunday school reflects what they are experiencing at home. I have had some pupils tell me in the middle of a message that they were hungry. Initially, I thought that they were simply seeking attention or lust-ing for the goldfish or M&M snacks in the snacks cabinet. No, they were not seeking attention. They were hungry. The more vocal one told me that he had not had breakfast, and then a couple of them echoed the same. Why would a parent send a child to a children's Sunday school without giving him breakfast? She probably did not have the means or time to make breakfast. A child acting up may simply be a way of expressing discomfort. In some cases, the children come from single-parent homes where the parent they are living with does two or three jobs to make ends meet. The children are left to raise themselves. There is no authority figure in the home, and adjusting to an environment where there are authority figures and structure is difficult for them. Children from dysfunctional homes tend to be bitter and withdrawn, and generally anti-social. There is another group of kids that prove difficult to manage in the class—siblings, especially if they are close in age. Fighting among siblings is often car-ried from home into the classroom, and they can wear the teacher down with their constant bickering.

A rowdy class is not a conducive environment for learning. Every teacher needs to maintain a firm control of his class. Knowing the backgrounds of the children in your class helps to understand where they are coming from. The teacher has two or three hours of contact time in a week with the children, and you cannot afford to spend half the time settling quarrels or attending to one child. Generally, children expect discipline in a classroom environment- whether in their regular school or Sunday school environment. However, how you handle discipline largely affects your effectiveness as a teacher. To start with, have at the back of your mind that discipline is not necessarily punishment. On rare occasions, negative reinforcement in terms of punishment may be necessary. There are people who advocate that punishment should never be employed. Some even suggest that time-outs should never be used. I totally disagree. When every other method fails, time-outs and reporting to parents may be our final resort. Discipline should be part of your lesson plan, and here are a few ways to take control of your class and maintain discipline.

1. Know your pupils by name: It is good practice to know the names of your pupils and *how to pronounce them* correctly. Your first interaction with a child is calling his name. You arrest his attention when you can call his name. The first day that I got to the Sunday school class in our current church, the substitute teacher who was teaching that morning

completed his lesson for the day before introducing me to the pupils. It was a noisy class, and the boys were particularly difficult. As I sat down, listening to the teacher and evaluating the environment, I quickly memorized the names of three of the boys who were disturbing the class and four of the girls who, for most of the time, were following the teacher and answering most of his questions. After introducing me to the pupils, the teacher allowed me a few minutes to say something to the children. I started by asking them questions, and the first pupil I asked a question was the most vocal in the class. I called his name as if I had known him for years. I remember the surprise look on his face. I proceeded to ask the other boys who were disturbing the class some questions and calling them by their names. As I continued speaking, I kept dropping the names of the girls that I had memorized. I praised them for being smart and listening. Without doing anything extra, the class became so quiet you could not recognize it as the same class that I met earlier. I taught them a song and hence introduced myself to the children in a way that they were not used to.

2. Know the parents of your pupils: Teaching children is like a pastoral ministry. You will be more effective as a teacher if you get to know the parents of the

children in your class and develop a relationship with them. Parents are a useful resource in controlling the behavior of their children in class. Your pupil will behave well in class if he realizes that you know his parents. My wife and I go the extra mile of visiting the families at home or inviting the children with their parents to our home for dinner. If you are single, I will caution that you handle visits with care. Relate more with the parent of a similar gender than the opposite until you establish a healthy relationship with the family. The same goes if your pupil has a single parent. Visit a single parent with your spouse, but if you are single, you may want to limit the interaction in church but make efforts to get to know them. When you are having difficulty handling a child in class, mere mention to the child that you may let his parents know about his behavior could be a deterrent. However, do not use that threat as the first line of action. In extreme situations, you may need to have a conversation with the parents, not necessarily to report a child but to work with the parents to resolve the issues that make him act up.

3. Define the boundaries: Some children like attention and will attempt to run your class. Create rules and let your class know ahead of time what is not acceptable and what the rules are. Repeat the rules as

often as possible. Some teachers would even write them out and post them on a board and let the class repeat the class rules loud a couple of times. From time to time, your class will get noisy. No teacher can avoid that, but how you control the noise matters. I allow my pupils time to play together and make some"healthy noise" because it is a time for them to bond with each other. If they are not disturbing the main sanctuary service and other classes, I allow them the "healthy noise" time. However, I do not tell them, "It's time for healthy noise." If you do, they will bring down the house. It develops organically and is often of tolerable limits. However, when we want to switch to more serious lessons, I will start a countdown—Five, four, three, two. Usually, before I get to one, the classroom is quiet. Any stray voice is shouted down by the other children. Among the pre-teens, cell phones constitute a huge distraction. They will claim that they use their cell phone Bible Apps to follow the lesson, which is true. Unfortunately, they do not stop at using the Bible Apps. They play games and surf the internet while in class. What we do is to provide a box or a secure place to put away all the cell phones at the beginning of the class. It is like a cell phone parking lot. We provide the pupils with Bibles and writing materials. When we are done teaching, or we want them to source information, we return their cell phones.

4. Time-Out: Warn a child that is disrupting the class and tell him the consequence of his behavior should he continue. I use time-out after the third warning. One-minute time-out for each year of the child's age is appropriate. If a child is five years old, five minutes of time-out is appropriate. If he is ten years old, let him stay away for ten minutes, during which you will have had enough time to take control of your class.

5. Earn the trust of your pupils: Welcome each child with a smile when they come to class. Call them by their names and ask them how their week had been. Show genuine interest in them and their world. If they start describing something that you know next to nothing about, like a video game move that they just learned, do not dismiss them offhandedly. Show some interest and ask them to explain the process. You will discover what makes them tick and start off a conversation from there. Do not dampen their enthusiasm without hearing them out. You can pick up something from the conversation that will help you guide the discussion to a more profitable end. As a coach, show them that you are knowledgeable and dependable. Understand their viewpoints and guide

them to sound Bible-based outcomes. Be prepared to answer questions on evolution, reproductive health, politics, and scientific concepts. Let the children see you as fair, kind, fun, a ready resource, repertoire of knowledge, and spiritual authority. They will respect you and respond positively to any disciplinary measures that you put in place.

6. Silence as a tool for discipline: When a child interrupts me while I am teaching or children are talking when I need their attention, I keep quiet to the point that my silence cuts through the cacophony with decisive demand for attention. Some teachers use a similar technique to force discipline in their classrooms. They whisper what they want to communicate, and the classroom quiets down. For me, I keep quiet, and the children follow suit, one after the other. Soon, there would be only one or two voices talking. When a child realizes that he is the only one talking and the entire classroom is quiet, he is embarrassed and will likely apologize. When they stop talking, I resume my lesson to emphasize the point that I kept quiet because they were interrupting me.

7. Change the seating arrangement: Three types of children interrupt the class the most when they sit together: (a) children who do not like each other, (b)

friends, and (c) siblings. When children are seated in a way that two or more who, for whatever reasons, do not like each other are close enough, conflicts from trivial things are inevitable. It could be something as trivial as one mistakenly putting a hand on another's notebook or thinking that her work is being copied by the other. For children who are friends, sitting together encourages chatting and bantering. Even when the teacher calls their attention and asks them to stop talking, they stop for a while until the natural urge grips them again. As for siblings, it is either they continue the conversation or the fight they started from home, or they keep needling each other. Separating them physically would ensure a better classroom atmosphere.

8. Give in-class assignments: As part of our lesson plans for any Sunday, I give the children a comprehension exercise which they must complete within a set time and turn in. Thereafter, I give them word search games or crossword puzzles to solve. The first three highest scores get prizes or are openly acknowledged. During the comprehension exercises, my classroom is like a college final examination in progress. Each child is working hard not only to get most of the answers correct but to beat the others in doing so. Since I do not announce the prizes ahead

of time and I do not give prizes every Sunday, the children take my assignments seriously.

9. Talk to parents when nothing works: There are some children who frequently interrupt the class or do not seem to be able to control themselves and may start a physical assault on other children. When it gets to that, I have a one-on-one session with the child, take the matter to the head of the children's department and when every intervention fails, report the development to the parents. In doing so, my goal is always to involve the parents in a strategy to redeem the child and not to punish him. Oftentimes the child is reacting to the circumstances of his family situation. One lady that I interviewed for my magazine told me how her preteen and teenage years were filled with suicidal tendencies because her parents were not together, and she wound up in foster homes. Dysfunctional families breed dislocated children. Divorce leaves children very bitter and emotionally fragile. Some children blame themselves and believe that they are the cause of their parents' divorce. Acting up in class is sometimes a way of crying out for help.

10. Take care of demonic operations: Most disciplinary issues that we are confronted with working with children are spiritual issues that need to be handled

spiritually. Think of it like this; you are pulling the children away from the kingdom of darkness into the kingdom of God. Do you think that you will be left to succeed without a fight from the kingdom of darkness? Certainly not. However, if the demons cannot get a direct hit at you, they will constitute themselves into nuisance factors to distract you from the great work that you are doing. If you do not recognize their works, they can easily take you on a ride chasing after shadows while wasting valuable time. Like I stated earlier, this is the reason that you need the gift of discerning of spirits. When demonic agents are at work, and you command them to cease, a certain calm that you cannot explain envelopes your class. It is a settled law; demons obey our commands. This emphasizes the need to be spiritually alert and prepared before you go to teach the children. If you know your authority and you exercise it, demons do not have a choice in the matter. They must obey. If you are ignorant of your authority, they will create real headaches for you. In the United States, some Christians that I have interacted with do not know about the operations of demons, and they attribute every behavioral issue that children display to neuropsychiatric problems. In Africa, on the other hand, most of these issues are regarded as demonic attacks. We need the Holy Spirit to help us recognize what disciplinary issues are simple behavioral problems and which ones are spiritual matters that need spiritual solutions.

6

Teaching Techniques

The right tools in our hands get the job done

Some churches are moving away from the traditional ways of teaching children in Sunday school to electronic platforms and technology-compatible teaching methods. However, some of these older techniques are time-tested and, in my opinion, are still useful even in the digital age. I will describe some of the commonly used techniques and comment on the newer models that are gaining attention.

Didactic teaching

The didactic method of teaching has been used for millennia. It is the lecture-style method in which the pupils are passive listeners and consumers of the instructions that come predominantly from the teacher or lecturer. The teacher is regarded as the expert and prime custodian of knowledge. Most times, the pupils do not challenge his authority or contribute to the instructions. Didactic teaching is mainly teacher-centered. Pupils take notes and answer questions. It is different from the open or experimental teaching styles in that it is structured. There is a curriculum that the teacher follows, which builds on the baseline knowledge that the pupil has on the subject. It adds one block at a time with the complexity of materials increasing, the higher the pupil progresses. For example, a math teacher does not expose the students to quadratic equations until they have learned simple and simultaneous equations. This approach helps the pupil digest the simple materials that would enable him to understand the complex materials when they are introduced down the road. It has been used in primary, secondary, and tertiary institutions for hundreds of years. Most Sunday school teachers also use this same method, although the degree of structure varies widely from one church to the other and from one teacher to another. In some churches, the children's Sunday school does not have a curriculum that the teachers use. Every teacher can make up their lessons on a Sunday-by-Sunday basis. There is hardly any continuity. That is why most children spend their time in the children's Sunday school learning about Noah and the Ark, David and Goliath, and the parable of the sower year after year. In other churches, the teachers use whatever curriculum that they find on the internet without following a defined structure. There is no road map as to what the children should be taught at each level. Consequently, there is no expected outcome as we transition the children from one class to a higher one. Although didactic approach to teaching has been used for hundreds of years, it is still effective in teaching children in this digital age.

Active learning (Problem-solving technique)

Have you considered that the body of knowledge that exists in any field today is an accumulation of different answers given to a myriad of questions asked by thousands, if not millions of people over the years on related subjects? Scientists, authors, journalists, judges, teachers, artists, weather forecasters, mechanics, and practically men and women in any profession keep asking the questions why, where, when, what, who, and how. Answers to each of these questions form the matrix on which a body of knowledge is built. When documented, others can read them and start asking questions from their own perspectives based on whatever information that they have been exposed to. This results in

143

the growth of knowledge in each field. A teaching technique that is gaining attention in recent times is the active learning or problem-solving technique in which the teacher poses a question, and the students work through them individually or as a group. Alternatively, the teacher will encourage the students to ask the questions, and all of them will work through and get the relevant answers. The teacher moderates a discussion on the subject and guides the pupils to a desired outcome. This is a method that I often integrate into my didactic teaching style. The teacher is both a teacher and a student when you use this method. While you are facilitating the discussion and steering it to the necessary outcome, you learn a lot from the pupils. We cannot afford to minimize the intellectual abilities of the children or the resources that they have been exposed to. Knowing that the children come from different backgrounds with varying resources in their experience, it is humble for the teacher to listen to the contributions of each pupil, sift the gem from the chaff, and synthesize an informed solution to the questions posed. I have found this method particularly useful in teaching my students in the following ways:

1. It helps the students to develop their critical thinking abilities: The children in our care are like tendrils of a climbing plant. The way you stake them helps the direction of their growth. If children are taught to memorize the multiplication table, for example, they

144

will easily memorize them by rote. However, if they are called upon to apply the knowledge, some may forget and get stuck. If, on the other hand, in addition to memorizing the multiplication table, the children are taught how to deduce the answers logically, solving mathematical problems that involve multiplication becomes easier. When they get into a bind, they can navigate their ways around the obstacle. If you were brought up learning Bible stories without applying the lessons of the story to your life, you are no better than a student studying Christian religious knowledge in college to complete his electives in order to graduate. You will have a head knowledge of the stories, but beyond that, you do not have a revelation knowledge which is what transforms lives. In using a problem-solving technique, you can ask a question like, "Can you name three Goliaths in your life?" Here the pupil is not asked to learn the story of David and Goliath alone; he is made to compare the giant Goliath with the giant issues in his personal life. He is made to think through that story. It comes alive. It pops up from the pages of the Bible to address issues that he is currently dealing with. It is no longer a story to memorize but a tool to address life's issues that he may confront.

2. It provides the teacher an opportunity to understand

the pupil's spiritual station: The responses that a child provides to a question will help the teacher gauge the child's spiritual maturity. In addition to the comprehension exercises that I give to my pupils, I always ask them to write down the insights they gained from the passage that I assigned them to read. The quality of the insights that each child provides is a pointer to his spiritual status.

3. It helps the child to gain a deeper understanding of the scriptures: By trying to come up with the answers to the questions, a child does a little more work than he would if all he does is just listen and take notes. In my experience, I have seen children research the subject matter on the internet to come up with the answers to the questions. When I give them take-home assignments, I intentionally allow them to involve their parents or anybody who could assist them in identifying the solutions to the problems. The idea is to expand their search horizons in providing a solution to a problem. In so doing, they gain greater insight and understanding of the subject.

4. It fosters collaboration and teamwork: Occasionally, we have the children work in groups to come up with solutions to the problems. While doing so, a couple of group dynamics become obvious. Natural leaders

emerge and take control. The more intellectually endowed may not be the leaders but have significant input in the final answers the team provides. Often, they would emerge as the secretaries to the team, documenting the consensus answers. The vocal and argumentative children try to have their way, but the intellectuals provide superior arguments to the contrary. This results in the group coming up with a qualitative solution to the problem. This collaborative effort generates team spirit, friendship, and bonding among the children, which could have a life-long impact on their spiritual growth and relationships.

In my opinion, the problem-solving or inquiry-based technique is not enough in communicating the gospel message to the children. However, when combined with other teaching techniques, its vibrant appeal creates an exciting atmosphere that enhances learning and retention. The children are empowered and involved in their own learning process, and the teacher generates a truckload of information that guides him in designing programs that are well targeted to the all-around development of the individual child.

"Gamification" technique

Games as a method of conveying academic instructions have been used for hundreds of years, but the addition of technology has reinvigorated it and has made the technique a vital tool that every teacher should be encouraged to use. Learning through play has become a more dynamic, fun, and vibrant classroom approach which engages the pupils in a way that is truly fun for them. Educational instructions are embedded in the games which the children play. Often, they do not realize that they are learning while playing the games. The evergreen exercise that goes with the song,

My head, my shoulder, my knees, my toes

My head, my shoulder, my knees, my toes

My head, my shoulder, my knees, my toes

They all belong to Jesus

is always fun to the children, but it has embedded in it a supreme message that every growing child should know—everything they have belongs to Jesus. While having fun trying to keep pace with the game, especially when the tempo is increased, the truth of the message is embedded in the subconscious mind of the child. One of the first songs that I composed for children is:

I am a child; Jesus loves me

I am a child; Jesus loves me

When I go to school, Jesus takes care of me

I am a child; Jesus loves me

Over the years, we created a dramatization of the song which children love. Again, increasing or reducing the tempo of repeat singing makes it real fun for the children. The object of the song, the love of Jesus, is burned into their psyche as often as they sing it or play the game.

In recent years, I have created word search and crossword puzzles for my pupils, which engages them while I am grading their comprehension exercises and before I present my lesson for the day. Embedded in these games are the lessons that I want them to take away from the passage I asked them to read. For example, if the lesson I want to emphasize is "Laziness is the highway to poverty," I would make the title of the word search "Laziness is the highway to poverty." Then I would create a word search that has words that relate to laziness, highway, and poverty. In the case of crossword puzzles, I put the letters and spaces and ask questions that will give them a clue while teaching them the lessons I want them to learn. For example, if I want them to insert the word laziness, I will give a clue like "another word for idleness" or "not willing to work." By the end of a given series of lessons, I would give my pupils jeopardy-like quizzes. It is fun, but the questions and answers are intentionally created to reinforce the teaching in class.

There are templates on the internet that you can use to create these games. Some of them are free, and others are offered for a subscription fee. All you need to do is to decide on the message that you want to emphasize and follow the instructions on how to create your own games. If you are unable to create and customize your own games, there are several age-appropriate Bible games on the internet that you can use.

Using drama sketches and songs

Just like in games, learning through drama sketches and songs is a vital tool that we can add to our toolbox. Unlike adults who can sit through a one-hour sermon, children have limited attention spans, and experts have advised that we engage them in multiple activities to sustain their interests. One way we have done this over the years is through drama sketches or skits. They form part of my lesson plan for each Sunday. Our approach has been to ask the children to come up with drama sketches that illustrate their understanding of the lesson for the day. Depending on the size of the class, the pupils are divided into two or three groups. We give them one theme based on the Bible lesson for the day or ask them to generate a theme for the drama sketch. Each group is given ten to fifteen minutes to come up with a skit. Occasionally, we allow them to appoint a team leader by themselves, but most times, we appoint the team leaders for the day. We monitor the progress of each team and make sure that all the children are participating one way or the other in the team project. After the practice period, they come back to present to the class. After the presentations, we ask two or three members of the opposing team to critique the performance of the team. This is the aspect of the exercise that I like the most. The unvarnished candor with which the children critique the performance of their opposing teams is a beauty to witness and a testament to an honest evaluation of a team's presentation. They score them highly if the opposing team does a good job. On the other hand, if the presentation is subpar, they do not feel bad stating so with disgusting scores. The personalities of the children also manifest when they critique their peers. Those who are easily satisfied will cheerfully score a presentation 98 percent, while the more critical ones while appreciating a great presentation may not go beyond 85 percent for the same presentation and would certainly defend their scores. One thing that I have learned over the years is that drama sketches are great ways of reinforcing the lessons. They help the children remember the central lesson you want them to take home. It is fun. They love it and learn while participating in it. If you are creating

151

the drama sketch, here are some suggestions.

- Have a definite message

- It must be action-packed

- Make it short and interesting

- Avoid violence

- Extol positive virtues

Songs are essential vehicles for conveying the gospel message to the children. The teacher needs to be intentional in selecting the songs to teach them. Depending on their ages, you may want to play a song for them and ask them to sing along or teach them the song and have them learn and sing together. Songs have been important components of our ministry to children. Vickie and I have written over 200 songs and produced two albums (CD) of some of our songs. In writing the songs, we have specific messages embedded in them. The children learn the songs and internalize the messages. For example, we composed this song to teach the children to share their gifts.

"Share what God has given you"
Share what God has given you

(Share, share, share)

Share your love with one another

(share)

Cast your bread upon the waters,

You will find it many days hence

Why not share the love of Jesus Christ, etc.

Let me give one more example of a song that we composed intentionally embedding a message that we wanted the children to learn.

"Jesus, I love you"

Jesus, I love you (oh yes, I do)

You're all the world to me (the world to me)

If all in life shall fail (in life shall fail)

I'll rest my hope in you (my hope in you)

You gave your all for me (your all for me)

Help me to do the same (to do the same)

And when I see your face

I'll say, Jesus, I love you

In recent years, some of our former pupils have been writing and asking me for the lyrics of the songs that we

153

taught them when they were young. They remember them but may have forgotten the full lyrics. Now that they have their own children, they want to teach them these songs that shaped their lives. We do not write songs for the sake of writing. They serve as vehicles to transport the godly messages we want ingrained in the lives of the children. Some people think that children cannot harmonize. That is far from the truth. If you train them to sing treble, alto, and tenor, they will harmonize well. Bass may be a stretch, but we have been able to pull it off. They enjoy harmonizing when they sing.

Using technology in the classroom

Over a career spanning thirty-three years in academia and on two continents, I have been privileged to teach university students either with little access to technology or some of the finest technology of the time. For many years, I taught students with chalk and wooden blackboard and did not have access to the internet. With time there was a gradual transition to teaching my students still using blackboards and chalk or whiteboards and dry erase markers combined with sending assignments to them and receiving completed responses by email. Later, I used the Blackboard Learn©. It is one of the few Learning Management Systems (LMS) used in higher institutions, corporate learning environments, and in some K-12 elementary school programs; it is the dream of any teacher. It is a highly integrated and interactive platform where both students and teachers have accounts that they access easily. It also has chat rooms for students to interact with one another and with their professors. Do we need such a highly sophisticated digital platform for teaching in children's Sunday school? My answer is, "Yes, why not?" If your church can afford it, it is a worthwhile investment towards the spiritual education of the children. I accept that it is expensive to run, and Blackboard does not offer its pricing publicly. However, there are other Learning Management Systems vendors that offer their pricing publicly. I believe that in the years to come, several LMS will be widely affordable. Remember how expensive the global positioning system (GPS) was when it was newly introduced into the market? You needed to shell out a lot of money to be a proud owner of this wonderful navigational system which commanded you nonstop, "In point two miles turn right, recalculating. In point seven miles make a U-turn." The first commercial model, NAV1000, had a price tag of $3000, and that was not long ago. The technology has advanced so much that your teenage sons will look at you as a dinosaur if you ever mention that you want to purchase a GPS (by the way, it costs about $68 on Amazon) when you have your smartphone in your pocket. Some cars have GPS now built-in as part of the infotainment systems that you see on the dashboard. Just like GPS technology, I believe that LMS technology will advance so much in the immediate future that it will be within the budget of most institutions and churches. It makes teaching a joy and learning fun.

In 2009, I had a major accident while playing soccer. The young men in my church in Chesapeake, Virginia, had scheduled a friendly soccer match with another church. I was not on the team but wanted to encourage them. I attended one of their practice sessions, and while we waited for the players to arrive, I decided to relive my younger years when I played soccer for my school team. I wanted to show off what we called "in-step" as I played with three of the team members who came early. It was a bad mistake. I hit my right foot on the ground and instantly broke three bones. Two surgeries and six months of not walking at all without orthopedic boots and a walker, and six additional months of not being able to walk again after the second surgery later, I hung up my soccer boots for good. I lived some forty-five minutes away from the institution where I was teaching pharmacology in a Pharmaceutical Sciences program which I was also coordinating. I needed to teach my classes but could not drive because of the injury. Somehow, we were able to get around that problem. My department was big on tele-education and video teleconferencing. With a camera mounted on my computer, I was able to teach my classes from home. Eleven years later, I would be teaching my Sunday school class from my living room via the Zoom video conferencing platform. This is the reality of the future. The technology is bound to get better and better, and I see a situation where it will be part of our regular instructional techniques. I recommend that every Sunday school teacher get familiar and comfortable with classroom use of videoconferencing technology. It is the future of teaching.

If there is one good thing that came out of the COVID-19 lockdown period for me, it was the fact that I learned to do video editing. I was in a bind. We had scheduled our children's day for June 18, 2020, and we were getting ready for the rehearsals when the pandemic hit with tornadic fury. With everyone in quarantine, the choice we had was to cancel the program altogether. It would have been perfectly understandable if we did. Somehow, while touching base, using FaceTime, and checking on how some of our pupils were doing, one mother informed me that her three boys created a skit. She recorded it and sent it to me. That gave me an idea. I asked her if the children could create a skit on the story of Jonah and the big fish, record and send it to me. What they produced was a masterpiece. The three boys Ugonna and his twin brothers Chuka and Chuma were superb. We then thought of getting most of the children in our Sunday school to do different activities at home. Their parents were requested to record them and send the videos to me. If we could find a video editor to stitch the videos together to form a continuous narrative and play the video during our children's day, we would have some fun and good lessons to learn for the day.

I got several videos from the parents, but how about a video editor? I had two of our former Sunday school pupils who do video editing as part of their jobs, but I could not muster the courage to send them the videos because the time was too short. Again, it was the election season, and one of them was handling technology for political campaigns. Asking him to do me that favor would be like David asking for water from the "well near the gate of Bethlehem" behind the enemy lines (2 Samuel 2; 15-17). I knew that he would oblige but at a great cost to his job. We had just about one week to get it done, and doing it commercially was beyond our budget. It was then that I learned that Joyce Bull, our church's communications director, could do some video editing. Joyce did the first editing, and it was great. However, more videos poured in from parents, and Joyce's work schedule would not allow her time to add them. I invested some money in subscribing to the editing Apps, went on YouTube, and spent hours learning how to do video editing using both *Kinemaster* and *Filmora* video editing suites. It was the best use of my time. I edited the videos according to the sequence we worked out and played it during our children's day. Personally, I found it rewarding, and I plan to invest in further educating myself to be more professional. The idea is that in the coming months, I plan to teach more people in our church how to do it and get professional-grade video quality.

That will also be part of our vacation Bible School activities in the coming years. I will then have the children make some amateur "movies" based on the lessons that we learned from class. Getting them involved in a creative process helps them to own that process. In doing so, they learn the lesson that you are trying to teach.

Visual Aids

It is generally believed that some people are auditory learners while others are either visual, reading/writing, or kinesthetic learners. Auditory learners are supposed to learn more by listening, while visual learners do better with pictures and charts. Reading/writing learners are more comfortable taking down notes and reading. Kinesthetic or tactile learners are hands-on learners who understand concepts better if they can participate in the learning process physically. The 44th and 45th presidents of the United States, Barack Obama and Donald Trump, are reported to represent the extremes of two of these profiles. President Obama was reported to be an avid reader (reading/writing learner) and preferred his daily briefings presented to him in tablets that he could read. On the other hand, it is reported that President Trump preferred in-person briefings with pictures and charts (visual learner). Preference is one thing, but actual learning is a totally different ball game. Scientific research has not shown that teaching in any particular way produces better learning outcomes in any of these groups. I may prefer to drink water with a particular cup, but that does not mean that if I drink water in another cup, I will not get the same results. The point I am making here is that while noting that some children may have their preferred learning styles, teachers should be creative in presenting their lessons in such a way that the pupils are able to retain the information better no matter the approach. Adding visual aids to our teaching helps sustain the interests of the children and expand their retention ability. A visual aid is an item that helps you illustrate your written or spoken information or convey what you are teaching in a way that can be seen and understood. It adds clarity to your instructions. There are different types of visual aids that you can use depending on the age group that you are teaching. Below are some of the commonly used ones:

1. Nature: I believe that the best visual aid to illustrate the story of creation is to take the pupils out and show them the beautiful plants and flowers, the hills and meadows, the animals, birds, and insects. The clouds, sun, moon, and stars. Nature speaks for itself. Show them the beauty of God's creation. It will help them understand your lesson better.

2. Pictures: Children enjoy looking at pictures, especially if they are colorful. It could be still pictures

or posters. However, I would caution that the teacher should properly vet the picture that you intend to use to illustrate your points or stories. We need to be mindful of what we expose the children to. I would rather talk to them without pictures if the pictures that I have are in any way graphic.

3. Videos: Videos and movies are the staples of this generation. You can access and use great videos on the internet, which will enhance the quality of your teaching. There are praise and worship videos. There are also instructional videos. There are cartoons and how-to-make-it videos all of which will create varieties in the quality of classroom environment that you can create. Again, a cautionary note about using videos: make sure you review them and determine that there are no offensive surprises tucked in somewhere in the middle. You cannot afford to show a video that has 99 percent excellent materials and 1 percent objectionable and damaging material to the children. So, *review every video on your own* before you show it to the children. Do not hop on the internet while in class and select a video that you have not had a chance to review. Any damage the video causes may be permanent.

4. Flannelgraph: Flannelgraphs or flannel boards are

pretty old storyboards that still have a place in Sunday school classrooms, especially for children in the lower classes. It is a board usually wrapped in flannel material and placed on an easel or hung on the classroom wall. Cutout pictures are placed on the board as the teacher tells a story. The characters in the story can be moved around by the teacher as he tells the story. Alternatively, an assistant can move the characters around while the teacher tells the story. The cutout pictures have flannel materials or other materials that make them stick lightly to the board. The story pictures come either cut out or in booklets from which you can cut them out, following the directions. There are videos on the internet on how to use them and a couple of websites, including the Child Evangelism Fellowship websites, where you can purchase them. They are inexpensive, and every church should be able to invest in them. They make storytelling come alive.

5. Puppets: Puppets have fascinated children for ages. Do you remember Maria and the von Trapp kids in the 1965 musical *Sound of Music*? There was a scene in which the von Trapp children under the direction of the tomboyish Maria presented a surprise show to Baron von Trapp and his guests. It was a highly choreographed and complex puppet show. Puppets

162

are human or animal-like objects which are manipulated by hand or rods and strings to produce actions representing what the puppeteer is saying. There are also video animations of puppets that have been used as educational or entertainment materials.

6. The puppet may be simple, like the finger or hand puppets, or complex like the marionette. The most used puppets are the finger or hand puppets. They thrill the children to no end. They fit readily into the children's world of fantasy. Creating and using puppets need some training. In the seventies, we used to organize weekend training workshops in puppetry, during which experts in puppetry trained our teachers on how to create and use different kinds of puppets. Technology has brought that training to your doorsteps. I will encourage all children's Sunday school teachers to use training videos on the internet and learn how to make and use the simple ones. For more creative teachers, I would suggest that you learn how to make the more complex marionette-type puppets. Work hard until you become really good at it. Then put up a show with your Sunday school children and have a relaxing evening event in your church. Everyone will be blessed.

7. Wordless Book: If you are interested in leading the

children to the Lord (every teacher should be), an effective way of doing so is to use the wordless book. It is called the wordless book, not as a metaphor but because there is literally no word in the book. It is a small book of colored blank pages. Each color represents a gospel message. Its history dates back to 1866, when it was said that the revivalist Charles Spurgeon first used it. Since then, children's ministry teachers and adults who are interested in leading children to Christ have found it a powerful tool in doing so. There are videos on the internet that can easily work you through how to use it in less than ten minutes to lead a child to Christ. If you have never tried it, please do so. The experience is highly rewarding.

Essentially, the different colors represent specific messages. The messages go something like this, "*Gold* represents heaven, and God wants us to go to heaven where the streets are made of gold, but we cannot get to heaven if we have sin in our lives which is represented by the *dark* pages. Since we have sinned and cannot get to heaven, Christ came to the earth to save us from our sin. He shed his precious blood on the cross and took the punishment that we deserved. *Red* reminds us of the precious blood of Jesus Christ with which He wiped our sins away, and the *white* pages remind us that when we accept Jesus into our hearts, He wipes our hearts clean, and then we can have the right to go to heaven. The book cover is *green* in color and reminds us of growth. When we give our lives to the Lord Jesus Christ, we need to grow." Many teachers over the years have used this little book. Give it a try prayerfully and see what the Holy Spirit can do with this simple tool in the life of a child.

7

Developing and Using a Curriculum

A map shows you where you are, where you are going, and how to get there

A curriculum is a guide or plan that the teacher uses to develop a day-to-day (or shall we say Sunday by Sunday) lesson plan for his children's Sunday school class. It is like a road map that envisions an outcome. Activities are then created to achieve that outcome. When I wrote about structure earlier, having a curriculum in a children's Sunday school class shows how seriously we take the assignment. Good writers do not start writing on a subject without first creating an outline which gives them a snapshot of how the narrative would turn out. If you do not have an outline, the story or article will not flow well. Similarly, a curriculum provides a plan of action. It states what you intend to archive and how you will go about achieving it. It follows a sequence in which one activity covered constitutes a springboard on which to reach the next goal. If the Sunday school teachers in one of the churches that I attended that I commented on earlier had an effective curriculum, they would not be teaching the children Christian apologetics without first leading them to the Lord and teaching t hem how to pray.

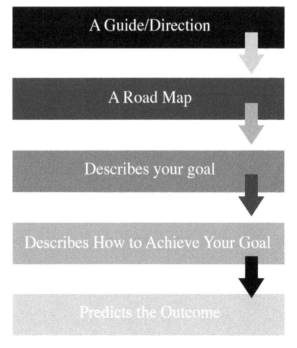

Your curriculum should describe your goal or objective, describe how to achieve it, and predict the outcome. There are many curricula on the internet, and some you can purchase from the bookstore. Please review them carefully before you adopt the one that you want to use. Otherwise, you may decide to develop your own curriculum. If you choose to develop a curriculum for your specific needs, here is one way to do it. Before you start, you may want to answer the following questions; (1) What is the age range of the pupils? (2) What is the intended outcome? (3) What message do you want to convey? (4) What time is available? (5) What are the resources available?

What is the age range of the pupils?

A good writer writes for his audience. Often, an author is tempted to massage his own ego by writing in a way that he personally enjoys consuming literature and not necessarily how his intended audience does. Some luxuriate in using highfalutin language and philosophical writing that gives them an air of superiority over their audience. Unfortunately, such literary malpractice endangers the purpose and lessons that the author wants to communicate. In a similar way, a curriculum that does not address the specific characteristics of the age group you are writing for is really not meant for that age group. I have described the curriculum that we used

169

in one of the pre-teens Sunday school classes that I was privileged to teach. We spent months teaching the children about
Christian apologetics as recommended by the curriculum.
We were three teachers in the class, and we took turns to
teach aspects of the lessons. When the time came for me to
teach, I wanted to know more about the children and started
by asking some of them to pray. I was shocked that only a
few of them could pray, and we were teaching them Christian
apologetics. We changed that curriculum eventually. For you
to realize the expected outcome in your curriculum, define
your audience from the beginning. What age group are you
creating the curriculum for? What are their characteristics—
how good is their attention span, how competitive are they,
can you use the active learning (problem-solving) format to
teach them, the didactic technique, or a hybrid of both? You
may need to do a little research to be able to answer these
questions.

What is the intended outcome?

Knowing where you are going makes it easy for you to
map out how to get there. A pilot does not set out flying from
London into the United States without knowing which city
he is flying to and exactly which airport that he would be
landing. Knowing that he is flying from London in Great
Britain to Reagan International airport in Washington, DC

helps the pilot to put up a flight plan that takes into consideration the optimal weather conditions along the flight path and alternate airports in case there is a weather-related event. He would also consider the number of passengers going on that flight, time of flight arrival to Washington, DC, and whether the flight is instrument flight rules or visual flight rules. The pilot factors all these into the flight plan before taking off from London. Your curriculum is like a flight plan, and so, the endpoint of the plan must be borne in mind and defined before you take off. Would you want the children to all have the opportunity of giving their lives to the Lord Jesus Christ by the time they go through the curriculum? Do you want them to be introduced to the baptism in the Holy Spirit, or do you simply want them to learn as many Bible stories as possible before they move to the next class level? Whatever outcome you expect should be decided on before you start writing down your curriculum.

What is your message?

The beauty of creating your own curriculum is that you can prayerfully decide on the overarching message that you want the children to be steeped in. If your emphasis is "the love of Jesus Christ has no geographical boundaries," you should create a theme that emphasizes that message. Every section of the curriculum should be written to reinforce that message in a sequential, coherent, and logical way. If your interest is to ensure that your pupils learn as many Bible stories as possible, it is beneficial to arrange them in such a way that either one central theme connects the stories or groups of stories are presented in a sequence that will emphasize related Bible principles. For example, if you want to share stories on kindness, you can share the stories of the good Samaritan, Jesus dining with Zacchaeus, Jesus feeding the five thousand, and Jonathan protecting David from Saul's anger and murder attempts. If you want any aspect of your curriculum to address fasting, you may arrange a sequence of stories that brings out fasting as the central message. For example, you may want to teach about Moses spending forty days when he went up the mountain to receive the ten commandments, Elijah escaping Jezebel after the showdown with the prophets of Baal, Esther fasting before speaking with King Ahasuerus, etc. Your curriculum should have a definite message.

What time is available to you?

In the flight plan analogy that I described earlier, the time of arrival at the pilot's destination was a critical component that must be considered. Here the time could be how many hours that a single Sunday lesson plan would last or how long a series of lessons would last. If you are working on a Sunday-by-Sunday plan, note that your plan should not be longer than the duration of the adult service in the sanctuary. No matter how exciting your lesson may be, your pupils are not independent. Often, they come to church with an adult who may be their parent, relative, or older sibling. Their time in church is thus regulated by the availability of the adult who brings them to church. Factor that in preparing your curriculum. The timing must be right. Do not forget that some of the adults that bring children to church go to work after church service, especially if they work in hospitals or other essential services.

It is a good practice to create your curriculum to have lessons taught in a series of different parts. For example, when I teach on faith, I may use one lesson to define faith, two to talk about examples of faith in the scriptures, and another one to talk about faith in contemporary Christianity. In doing so, I structure my curriculum to use four Sundays to teach the children about faith. A series on the whole armor of God (Ephesians 6:10-17) can take all of six weeks. If you are preparing a curriculum that will last for six months or one year, you may choose to work on multiple topics. One more thing that we should keep in mind while developing our curricula is that the children have limited time to spend in the children's church. We should design curricula knowing that, unlike the adult church, we may not have them for more than five years. For some children, it is as short as one or two years, depending on when their parents or the adults that bring them to church join or leave the church.

What resources are available to you?

All churches do not have the same or even similar resources. Some may be financially endowed and therefore are able to provide for the needs of their children's departments. Others are praying hard for a similar grace. Before writing your own curriculum, it is wise to consider what resources are available to your children's ministry in terms of personnel, financial and infrastructural endowments. It would not be realistic to write a curriculum that emphasizes video sessions or occasional movies to augment the teaching if you do not have a television monitor or a computer. If your church does not have internet connections, all that we have been talking about children's ministry in a digital age may sound like fables and mirages to you. You will need to be creative with your curriculum in such a situation and come up with realistic approaches that will serve your peculiar situation well. While writing, you may need to double-check the Bible stories that you want to use. A Bible, books, a Bible concordance, dictionary, and cross-references would be helpful. Do not forget that the internet is a vast repertoire of resources. You will find an answer to almost every question you may ask on the internet. However, remember that not everything on the internet is genuine. There is a lot of garbage out there. You will need to sift through them to find the gem that you are looking for.

Prepare your own curriculum

Having addressed the questions above, you have the materials that you need to write your curriculum. I would then recommend that you take the following steps in developing your curriculum.

- Prayerfully decide on the object lesson.

- Find scriptural stories that support the lesson.

- Ask the following questions:

    - What is the story about?

    - Who is the story about?

    - What lessons/insights do you gain from the story?

    - How does the story help the child's walk with the Lord?

- Get the Bible passages relevant to the object lesson ready.

- Decide on what technique and props you will use.

- Find a standard curriculum and use it as a template.

- Write your curriculum.

- Review your curriculum and check for accuracy of the information.

- Rewrite aspects of the curriculum for clarity or accuracy.

- Use your curriculum.

175

8

Leading a Child to Christ

I plant my feet in His footsteps whilst holding a child's hand

One of the greatest joys of a teacher in the children's ministry is to lead a child or a group of children to Christ. It is common to assume that every child under our tutelage is born again. At times, this may be true, but most times, it is wishful thinking. Much of it is out of a defense of our ego than a commitment to have the children in our class committed to the Lord. Let me explain. It is a kind of bragging right to say that "Since I have been teaching a cohort of children for one year, they have all been born-again" because the converse is a damning testament of our ineffectiveness. However, our number one job is to lead them to Christ. We need to get into that business more seriously. Whatever else we are doing in the children's ministry that does not lead the children to Christ and disciple them for His glory, as I stated earlier, is mere social entertainment.

Often, we are not able to achieve this primary job description of ours because we do not know how to do it, or we are afraid of failure. However, the good news is that studies have shown that more born-again Christians gave their lives to the Lord as children (eighteen years and under) than as adults (more than eighteen years). We have an audience that is pure and trusting, gentle in spirit, and dependent on us to guide them through life. It makes sense that they will follow what directions we give them when they can see the genuineness of our actions. They see us as the default role models that they should follow. If we present the gospel to them and explain to them what it really means to give their lives to Christ, most of them will. One thing that we should note is that it is not our job to convert the children. It is the work of the Holy Spirit. Ours is to introduce them lovingly and intentionally to the Lord. If we do that on a weekly basis, we will have done our jobs.

If you intend to lead one child to the Lord, you may start by showing interest in what he is doing or the specific strengths that he has exhibited in class. You may even start a conversation by asking him how he is doing at school, especially if he is the smart one. For children that are struggling with their academics, you need to be extra sensitive if you decide to use this approach. Otherwise, they will shut down and simply wish that you get lost. You may start a conversation with a child by saying, "Laurie, tell me your favorite subject at school and why it is your favorite." This is an open-ended approach that encourages the child to talk rather than give one-word answers. Laurie will be willing to share with you a subject that she is most at home with. "I love social studies because I am exceptionally good at it. My social studies grades are always good. I had four As in the past four tests that we did in social studies." Volunteering that information means that she is expecting some compliments. Make sure you seize the opportunity and compliment her. "Excellent, you are smart! Please keep it up." Now you can go on and ask her more questions, the answers of which you expect her to show off her successes. "I am sure you are good in other subjects." Laurie will volunteer the information, "I am quite good in English, music, and history, but my math is not so good. At times I make a C or B in math." There is a fork at this juncture. You may either pursue the positive track or the negative track. Each track will lead you to the same result. Let us consider the positive track first. She has offered information that suggests that she is well at home with social studies, English, music, and history, which suggests that she is at home with the arts rather than science at this stage. You may then ask, "What career would you like to pursue in life?" "I would like to be a lawyer or journalist." The rest of the conversation may then go something like this:

You: Sounds good. After that, what will you like to do?

Laurie: I will work in the State Department.

You: I am so proud of you. You have already figured it out.

Laurie: Yes, I have. My dad works in the State Department. He is a lawyer and a

journalist.

You: Oh, I see. You want to follow the footsteps of your dad?

Laurie: Yes, I do. He is very smart.

You: Wonderful. You know, the way that you want to follow in the footsteps of your

father, Jesus wants you to follow in his footsteps too.

Laurie: How do I follow in Jesus' footsteps?

At this point, Laurie has opened the door for you to come in and share the gospel with her. You can proceed in ten to fifteen minutes to share the gospel as simply as you can. Show her the scriptures that say that she is a sinner and sinners do not have a part with the Lord Jesus Christ until they repent. Tell her that all sinners will go to hellfire when they die or when Jesus Christ comes back to the earth. Tell her that she needs a savior since she cannot save herself. Tell her that the only person who can save her from going to hell is Jesus Christ. That is why he came and shed his blood. Finally, tell her that she must receive Jesus Christ into her heart for her to be saved. At this point, you will need to explain to her what salvation means. Invite her to give her life to the Lord. Pray the sinner's salvation prayer with her. Assure her that if she repented and prayed the prayer from her heart, she is saved.

On the other hand, if you want to pursue the negative track, your conversation can go something like this.

You: It sounds like you have a problem with Math, right?

Laurie: Yes, I do. I do not know why it is too hard. I think I can never make more than a

C in math—ever.

You: Do you remember what Philippians 4:13 says?

Laurie: Yes, I do.

You: Could you please tell me what it says?

Laurie: Yes. It says I can do all things through Christ who strengthens me.

You: Which part of that statement is not correct?

Laurie: I guess none.

You: Then you can do all things, including math, correct? It sounds like you can get an A

 in Math.

Laurie: No—never!

You: Does Christ strengthen you?

Laurie: I am not sure.

You: By the way, do you have a relationship with him? Are you born again?

Laurie: I am not sure.

You: Would you like to be born again?

Laurie: Yes, but how can I be born again?

At this point, you are invited to share with Laurie how she can be born again. The conversation may not go exactly as suggested here, but you can direct it to the point where

Laurie gets interested in knowing how to be born again. That is the goal. You do not waste the opportunity. Go ahead and lead the child to Christ. A much easier way is to use the wordless book. One advantage the book has is that it creates curiosity instantly, and you can dive into the later part of the discussion without waiting for the opening. The discussion can proceed like this.

You: Hi Laurie, I have a tiny little book I will like you to see (you hand her the book).

Laurie: This looks like a book, but it has no words—only colored pages.

You: You are right. It is called the wordless book. It shows you how you can go to heaven.

Laurie: How?

You: Okay, let me show you. Are you interested?

Laurie: Yes, I am.

You have arrested Laurie's attention. You can then go on and share the gospel with her, following the method that I described earlier. When you are done, ensure that the child says the sinners' prayer as you lead her to Christ. Seize the opportunity and make sure you *seal the deal*. It looks simple, and some teachers may not believe in its efficacy, but it

183

works. Recently, I had the good fortune of inviting one of my former students to speak to my Sunday School class during one of our Zoom hangout sessions. I knew that she was born again in our Sunday school when she was young, but I did not know exactly when and how. While ministering to the children, Dr. Kemi Ogunsan shared with them the story of how she got born again. She told them that she was ten years old when she received the Lord as her personal Lord and Savior. She confirmed that it happened when she was in our children's Sunday school at the University of Ife in Nigeria. She told my pupils that it was not me that led her to the Lord but another teacher in our Sunday school. The teacher used the wordless book to lead her to the Lord. Kemi has been a medical doctor for more than twenty-eight years and oversees the children's ministry in her church. She is also the wife of the pastor of New Covenant Church in Hyattsville, Maryland. Years ago, she raised and conducted one of the largest mass choirs on a university campus. You can trace her life accomplishments and service to the Lord to that day when a caring Sunday school teacher used a simple instrument called the Wordless Book to lead this ten-year-old to the Lord. That teacher may never know that the seed that she sowed has grown into this mighty oak tree which has birthed many oak trees that are providing direction, protection, and hope to this generation. When she gets to heaven, this teacher will be surprised to see a star on her crown representing the ten to fifteen-minute service she did by leading Kemi to the Lord.

In this discussion, I have focused on leading one child to the Lord to emphasize how important a single child is to Him. However, we are blessed to have the opportunity to multiply the effects of our efforts by leading many children to the Lord at the same time. As we minister to the children every Sunday, let us make it a habit to give them the opportunity to give their lives to the Lord. It may sound redundant, but you may not know which of the children will be ready on any given Sunday to accept Christ. Some of them will do it as often as you make the altar call. That is okay. Allow them to move at their pace. Along the way, they will understand what they are doing and take a definite stand for the Lord. This emphasizes the need for every teacher to prepare well before you teach the children. Prepare as if there is a child that would be in church for the last time every Sunday. Bathe yourself in prayer and the presence of the Holy Spirit before you teach. Prepare as if your pastor gave you the assignment to preach to your local assembly on a given topic. That level of intensity is needed for you to be effective. I must acknowledge that routine can get in the way of adequate preparation for us but let us be vigilant because that may be a way the devil will use to water down our focus and message. I spend most Saturday evenings preparing for what I will teach the children on Sunday and remain sensitive to the Holy Spirit whenever I am teaching. The bottom line is that we need to make it a priority to lead the children to the Lord, no matter what topics we are teaching.

The Children Evangelism Ministry in Nigeria has been remarkably effective in reaching out to children because of its concentration on leading a child to the Lord. The leadership of that ministry has been laser-focused on that one mission for more than forty years. The ministry has grown astronomically from when it started in Ife in 1979 to branches in thirty-six states and the federal capital territory Abuja in Nigeria and some other countries. It even has a ministry headquarters in Ilorin, Nigeria. The president of the ministry Brother Egbuna Chukwudile has not veered from the vision. There are hundreds of Nigerian Christians today who can associate their coming to the Lord and Christian upbringing to the ministry of CEM. Only eternity will reveal the impact of this ministry and similar ministries like the Child Evangelism Fellowship on the Christian lives of thousands of people all over the world.

9

The Holy Spirit in Children's Ministry

Let the Pentecostal fire fall; allow the supernatural a position of preeminence

In the summer of 1974, I attended an open-air meeting (we called it an open-air crusade in Nigeria) in the commercial city of Aba in eastern Nigeria. That meeting changed my life for good. It was organized by the late Morris Cerullo's World Evangelism Ministry. We attended the meeting for three nights in a soccer stadium that held thousands of people. The venue was packed night after night by people who came with sick relatives, needed a miraculous touch of God in their lives, or were simply curious specta- tors and critics. The power of God was on public display in that meeting. I saw people who were brought into that venue on wheelchairs and others with crutches stand up and walk. Blind people received their sight, and all manner of diseases were healed as the worship led by Alexander Ness proceed- ed or soon after Evangelist Morris Cerullo got on stage and started speaking. There was something I noticed about that meeting. The Holy Spirit was given an uncommon place in it. He was upfront, and regrettably, that has not been His place in most churches. This is what I mean. In most churches, we talk about our church buildings and idolize our pastors and founders. We revere them as if they are not mortals. We spend so much time arguing about tithes and prosperity mes- sages. Even pastors talk about the church as "my church" as if it is their personal enterprise. We do not recognize the presence of the Holy Spirit. Pastors and preachers headline our activities, and the Holy Spirit is given a back seat. Is it any wonder the power of the Holy Spirit is scarce in our churches? During this meeting, Alexander led tens of thou- sands of people in that soccer stadium in worship. This song was sung over and over as the atmosphere got charged with the tangible presence of the Holy Spirit. The crowd was hun- gry; the people were expectant. They came for the solutions to their physical and spiritual problems, and as the worship ascended to heaven, the blessings poured on all that were present like a tropical rain. Miracles upon miracles filled the air. The song was:

Come Holy Spirit; I need you

Come Holy Spirit, I pray,

Come in your strength and your power,

Come in your own gentle way

Each time Morris Cerullo came onstage, he started by asking the crowd to keep quiet because the Holy Spirit was in the place. That was a mark of honor to the Holy Spirit. Sure enough, He was there. The sound of the silence was palpable, and soon, you would hear somebody screaming for joy, a quadriplegic just walked off his wheelchair, a blind child just received his sight, etc. It went on for the three nights that we attended the "crusade."

Miracles happened because the Holy Spirit had a front seat in the meeting. Miracles will happen in our Sunday school classes and children's ministries when we open them up for the Holy Spirit. In a digital age, when everything seems to move at the speed of light and electrons and we can do drive-by prayer sessions, we need to invite the Holy Spirit back into the church. We need the Holy Spirit in our classrooms. His presence makes a huge difference. Most of the children we are teaching have not experienced the power of God and need to. When they do, they will run with it for most of their lives thereafter. Therefore, as children's ministry teachers, our priorities should be to lead the children to the Lord, followed by introducing them to the baptism of the Holy Ghost. I will devote the rest of this chapter sharing testimonies of our experiences when we did what I am suggesting that you do.

Thirteen years without teaching about the Holy Spirit

I gave my life to the Lord after hearing a salvation message during a Scripture Union meeting in my secondary school in 1972. I did not answer the altar call during the meeting but could not shake off the message from my mind. At home, I knelt beside my bed and surrendered my life to the Lord. A couple of months later, the Lord led me to work with children. I enrolled for my first degree at the University of Ife in 1975, about two and a half years after I had given my life to the Lord. After graduating in 1979, I proceeded to do my graduate degrees and worked in the university for another ten years, making a total of fourteen years three months that I spent in the university community. I worshipped at All Souls Chapel in the university and was a children's Sunday school teacher in the chapel from September 1975 till January 1990 when we left Ife. From 1972 till 1985, I did not teach the children about the Holy Spirit. That means that for the three years prior and all the ten years that I spent in the university till 1985, I did not teach the children about the Holy Spirit. Part of the reason, as I mentioned earlier, was that we did not have the topic in our curriculum, but a more important reason was that I was not baptized in the Holy Spirit in the early seventies, and therefore I could not give what I did not have. When we got baptized in the Holy Spirit, we were careful not to upset the traditional chapel setting in case the children "misused the Holy Spirit." Looking back on that chapter of my life and service to the Lord, I regret that we did not lead the children we taught all those years to that Pentecostal experience. When we finally did, the difference in the outcomes of our service (from a human perspective) was glaring!

The outpouring of the Holy Spirit

I have written some of the stories that I am about to share here in my earlier book *God knows my house number*. However, they have even greater relevance to the current narrative that I believe they are worth repeating. Two remarkable things happened to me in 1985. I got married to Vickie, and the Lord visited us at home. One day, Vickie was alone in the house after our wedding. It was time for her usual quiet time in the afternoon, a time that she set apart every day to study the scriptures and pray. She felt the presence of someone in the room with her but could not see the person. Shortly after, she heard the voice of the Lord, telling her to get her Bible which was in our bedroom. After she got the Bible, the Lord gave her a passage to read, which according to her, summarized some thirteen instructions and promises He had given her earlier for our married life. The Lord asked her to share them with me when I came back from the laboratory. We call these instructions the road map for our married life. One of the things which He said that bears relevance to the current narrative is that we should open our clenched fists because He wanted to put some work in our hands. We obeyed, and He has given us several assignments since then.

To start off, He showed up in our Sunday school class and set off a revival that touched so many children and the youth in the university staff quarters. As I mentioned in the introduction to this book, I had taught children in the Sunday school in All Souls Chapel in the University of Ife for ten years without teaching them about the Holy Spirit, largely because of self as well as it not being in our curriculum. When the time was ripe, the Holy Spirit started the conversation through the mouths of two of the children. In response to a question I asked them concerning the topics they would want us to teach them the following year, one of the children asked me why we did not teach them about the Holy Spirit.

Another one echoed the question and said, "Yes, Uncle, why don't you teach us about the Holy Spirit?" I heard it clearly, and I knew who was asking me the question. God was using the children to rebuke me for keeping such an important topic from them.

Vickie and I spent the next six weeks teaching the children about the Holy Spirit. We did not have the resources that we have today. We did not have access to the internet like we do today. However, we had Dake's Annotated Bible with commentaries and cross-references. That was a useful resource. We were able to study and teach the children about the person and work of the Holy Spirit in the Old and New Testaments. We taught them about the gifts of the Holy Spirit and told them that those gifts were not for the early church alone. The gifts were also for them. The six weeks of systematic teaching on the Holy Spirit laid the foundation for the conflagration that followed and the revival that hit the children and youth in the university campus community. We invited Dr. Kehinde, a professor of electrical engineering who led a vibrant Pentecostal fellowship on campus, as a guest speaker to speak to the children about the Holy Spirit. I remember that when I reached out to him, he accepted our invitation but requested us to pray for God to give him the wisdom to be able to explain it well to the children. Dr. Kehinde is a firebrand preacher and teacher of the word of God, but he shared a similar sentiment that I had before the Lord jolted me to reality. He, too, expressed the concern that the subject was a bit advanced for the children. I told him that I understood what he said and that we would pray for him. When he spoke to the children, he used illustrations upon illustrations to simplify the subject for them.

After the six weeks of laying the scriptural foundation, it was time for the practical manifestation of all that we had been teaching them. One of the children, Joke Ademosun, was going back to boarding school in a different city and needed this supernatural experience we had talked about for six weeks. After church service, she asked Vickie to pray for her to receive the baptism in the Holy Spirit. Vickie did, and she received the baptism with the evidence of speaking with an unknown tongue. The news of her Holy Ghost baptism experience spread among the children. The following Sunday, two other girls also asked Vickie to pray for them to receive the baptism in the Holy Spirit. She did, and they were baptized in the Holy Spirit, with the evidence of speaking in tongues.

Mass deliverance and Holy Spirit baptism

Our Happiness Club meeting was held every Saturday between 4 p.m. and 6 p.m. at the university staff school. We got to the school for one of our meetings during the revival and saw a class full of pre-teen boys and girls, and teenagers. There were probably up to forty young people in that classroom. I thought that they were all there for our practice. When I asked, one of them told me that they were waiting for my wife. Someone in their school had spread the news that she was praying for children to receive the Holy Spirit and was conducting deliverance. I took the younger children to my class while Vickie, assisted by Funke, handled the group. Many of the children received the baptism in the Holy Spirit and spoke with unknown tongues. There were also express manifestations of demons as Vickie prayed for some of the children and cast them out. Some wriggled on the floor like snakes while others just fell down and remained on the spot as she commanded the demons out of the children. Some of the children were excited about what they saw. It was practical. It was real. There was a supernatural visitation. What we had spent six weeks teaching them was real.

When we got to the staff school the following Saturday for our weekly Happiness club meeting, the news of what happened the previous Saturday had gone into the city, and we had young people from secondary schools outside the university campus waiting to receive the baptism in the Holy Spirit or deliverance from demons. The classroom was full, and demons manifested as they were cast out of the children. The children who needed baptism in the Holy Spirit spoke in unknown tongues as evidence of receiving the baptism.

Unfortunately, we took an action that, in retrospect, I think we should not have taken. Happiness Club is the activity arm of All Souls Chapel Children's Sunday school. The chapel consisted of the mainstream Protestant churches like Anglican, Baptist, Methodist, Presbyterian, etc. For all the years I attended church service before this revival, I never heard any preacher preach on the baptism of the Holy Spirit in the chapel. We were not sure how the church leadership would view what was happening in our Happiness Club meetings. We did not want to upset the clergy. After the third week of this wave of Pentecostal experience, we decided to stop the mass deliverance and Holy Spirit baptism. Instead, we announced that we would be handling individual cases. Ironically, one of the pastors in the chapel's leadership team brought his children on that Saturday for deliverance, and as the demons were cast out from his children, they exhibited the typical manifestations as they left these young people. I believe that a lot more children would have been delivered from demonic oppression, and many more could have received the baptism of the Holy Spirit if we had not stopped prematurely.

Gifts of the Holy Spirit

For the first time in ten years, what happened in my class on this Sunday morning was spectacular. I do not remember how many weeks had passed, but it was certainly after we had finished teaching the children about the Holy Spirit. Our class was on the third floor of this all concrete Department of Agricultural Economics building, and worship time for us was a special event every Sunday. Our chapel building project was in progress off Road One, about halfway of the three-mile stretch between the university gate and the administrative buildings. The Faculty of Agriculture had hosted the chapel for so many years, and its administration had been magnanimous to the chapel by allowing us to use their foyer as our "sanctuary" and classrooms for the children's Sunday school. There were few academic activities on campus during the weekends, and so, the sound of our worship did not constitute much nuisance to the staff and students of the faculty. We had practically unlimited freedom to worship the Lord the way we pleased. On this day, our worship had a peculiar heavenly ring, and the Holy Spirit visited us in a special way.

I was leading the worship and what happened was like our own upper room experience. As the praise and worship poured out of the mouths and hearts of these young ones, you could feel the anointing in the room. The presence of the Holy Spirit was not mistakable. While the worship was going on, I felt led in my spirit to ask one of the girls to pray. As she opened her mouth to pray, she started speaking in tongues. That was the first time in my ten years as a Sunday school teacher in this university chapel that any child would speak in tongues during our worship. It was so beautiful. She prayed in this glorious heavenly language for a while and stopped. We continued with our worship. Again, when I had a nudge in my spirit, I tapped a boy on his shoulder and asked him to pray. Just like the girl did, as the boy began to pray, he started speaking in tongues. The children were ecstatic. They were seeing the proof of what we had been teaching them for six weeks. They asked more questions, and we explained to them what they just witnessed. That was the beginning. In the weeks and months to follow, we had an outpouring of the Holy Spirit in a measure that we had never experienced before. Ministries were born, several gifts of the Holy Spirit were manifested by the children, and a revival broke out among the children and youth living on the university campus staff quarters. Even children in the elementary and secondary schools on the University of Ife campus were impacted by the revival.

"They will call me pastor"

One thirteen-year-old boy, Temi Odejide, told us a story that has stayed with me all these years. He said that he was going to school one morning during this revival and heard the Lord tell him to preach to members of his class before the lessons started. He was afraid to do so. He tried to find an excuse and told the Lord that his classmates would call him pastor. He said that what surprised him was that when he got to school and asked his classmates to sit down for his message, they all complied until he was done giving them the gospel message. When he finished, they called him "pastor." However, it did not matter anymore. He obeyed the Lord, and God used him as an instrument to sow the seed of salvation in the hearts of his classmates. As the day wore on, God allowed him to experience a supernatural intervention that changed the trajectory of his life, career, and ministry. In the afternoon of that same day, one of the girls in the school took ill. Some of the students who heard him preach in the morning came to him and asked him to pray for the girl. He did, and the girl got well. Thereafter, he became an authentic "pastor" for his classmates. He started a fellowship in school, which later moved to his father's garage in the university quarters. He called it Anointed Fellowship. Young people flocked to his fellowship, and I believe that the ministry path he followed later in life was paved by the experience he had leading a flock of more than thirty teenagers and pre-teens in his fellowship. They witnessed to their friends, prayed for the sick, cast out demons, and prayed for baptism in the Holy Spirit for their peers. Temi is now a medical doctor and a pastor. He pastored a big church in Nigeria and is currently pastoring a church in London.

Sola spoke French

There is a story in Matthew 8:10 where Jesus commented on the faith of the centurion who asked Jesus to just give the command and his dead son would live. Jesus said, "Assuredly, I say to you, I have not found great faith, not even in Israel."

This was the kind of faith that Sola and Dehumo expressed when they burst into our Sunday school class one morning during the revival and asked Vickie to pray for them for deliverance and baptism in the Holy Spirit. They were thirsty. They were hungry for this supernatural experience. They could not wait, and the huge downpour could not stop them. There was a huge tropical rain on the university campus that morning. I was teaching when these two boys came to our class and straightaway went to Vickie and asked if she could minister to them. Vickie told them that it was raining and there was no classroom nearby where she could minister to them. The boys would not take no for an answer. They took off in the rain to scout for an empty classroom. When they came back, Vickie followed them and prayed for them to receive the baptism in the Holy Spirit. They did. Vickie told me that Sola spoke in French when he received the baptism of the Holy Spirit. Of the three of them in that room that morning, it was only Vickie who could speak and understand French.

Witnesses go in twos

We did not instruct them on what to do concerning witnessing. However, I believe that along the way, the children learned that they were supposed to be witnesses when the Holy Ghost came upon them, as the early disciples did. As the revival moved beyond the four walls of our chapel into the city, some of the children in the elementary school (university staff school to be specific) organized themselves in twos. Each group decided who would go out to witness to other children in their class during their lunch break and who would stay back praying. These eight to twelve-year-olds reported to us that they preached to other kids and laid hands on those who needed baptism in the Holy Spirit and prayed for them.

There are many more testimonies of the acts of the Holy Spirit during this revival that the current narrative will not accommodate. Most of the children in our Sunday school class got baptized in the Holy Spirit with the evidence of speaking in tongues. From then on, some of the children gave prophecies during our programs and outreaches that were right on the mark. The children prayed for the sick amongst themselves or at school, and they recovered. The glory of the Lord descended on the university campus quarters' children and youth. Young people traded their mischief for evangelism and ministry. The older children established new ministries like The Beacons, Quarters Christian Youth, etc.

I have used these examples to illustrate what happens when we give the Holy Spirit the front seat in our children's Sunday school. No matter what educational techniques we use, we are more effective when we give the Holy Spirit His place in the lives of the children. One advantage we have doing that is that the Holy Spirit will guide us and the children in such a way that we easily recognize the work of Satan and demons in our environments. There is a misconception that I have observed among some Christians in America. Some think that demons exist only in Africa and some developing nations of the world like Brazil and India but not in the United States.

Dear teacher, if that is what you believe, that is the lie of the devil. Please disabuse your mind of that way of thinking because it will hinder you from appreciating your need and the need of the children that you teach for the baptism in the Holy Spirit and enduement with power. The scripture says in Ephesians 6:12, "For we do not wrestle against flesh and blood but against principalities, against powers, against the rulers of the darkness of this age, against spiritual hosts of wickedness in the heavenly places" (NKJV).

If the devil succeeds in making you comfortable with him, you have lost your bearing. If he can convince you to believe that demons do not exist in the United States or developed countries of the world, then he has succeeded in diminishing the reason for you to prepare the children against the hosts of darkness that are unleashed against them and the need to have them baptized in the Holy Spirit. We attended a children's ministry training a few years ago in which the speaker stunned some of us by what she said. We had had great sessions listening to her speak on a variety of subjects. The training was scheduled for six weekends of six hours every week. She poured into us useful insights and approaches to children's ministries. My wife and I enjoyed her presentations and endeavored to be present in all the sessions. During one of the sessions, she said something to the effect that teachers should be prepared every Sunday to reach out with the gospel to the children because we would not know if that would be their last day in the Sunday school.

In support of her view, my wife contributed by telling the class that she personally prepared for every class during the Wednesday mid-week services in our church, as if she would meet a child who she would have only one opportunity to minister to and never see again. She then told a story of a girl who came to her class only two times and never came back. On the second day, the girl told her that someone she described as a big man visited her room often through the window since her mother bought her a "dream catcher." She was the only one who saw this person. Vickie recognized the demonic oppression the girl was suffering and prayed a prayer of deliverance for her. It turned out that it was the last day that her grandmother brought her to the church. The girl never came to the church again. The speaker turned to Vickie and asked, "Was that in Africa?" to which Vickie replied that it was in our church right there in Virginia. Then the speaker asked Vickie if the girl was an African. I saw the uncomfortable looks on the faces of our fellow teachers who were attending the training. Vickie and I were the only Africans in the class that day. "No, she is a Caucasian American," Vickie replied. Then came the bombshell. "No, no, no, those things don't happen in America. It is only in places like Malawi you hear such stories," our speaker said.

The room froze in incredulous silence. During the break, some of the teachers came over to our seats in what looked like a solidarity rally. One teacher told us that her father was involved in Teen Challenge ministry and that growing up, she saw her father cast out demons from Americans and set them free from demonic oppression. Even if the demons working in Americans appear "respectable," that is their cover. They are still demons, and we need to identify them and cast them out, no matter how much they disguise their appearance. It is the Holy Spirit who reveals their true identity.

Ministering baptism in the Holy Spirit

After the death, resurrection, and ascension into heaven of our Lord Jesus Christ, the church comprised a timid and powerless band of disciples who were games for the persecuting authorities. Some were martyred, and others hid themselves from the marauding agents of the state. However, on the day of Pentecost, a supernatural boldness was infused into the disciples by the Holy Spirit, and a huge revival broke out in their numbers. They set off a chain of conversions that the devil and his cohorts could not stop till this day. In centuries following the Pentecost, revival has come in waves, and God has used individuals who received a revelation knowledge of what the Holy Spirit could do if we yielded to Him to spearhead these revivals. We have heard about the praying Hyde, Kathryn Kuhlman, Martin Luther, Charles Spurgeon, Reinhard Bonke, etc. However, the Spirit of God, speaking through prophet Joel, says, "And it shall come to pass afterward that I will pour out my Spirit on all flesh. Your sons and daughters shall prophesy, your old men shall dream dreams, your young men shall see visions, and also on My menservants and on My maidservants, I will pour out My Spirit in those days" (Joel 2: 28-30, NKJV).

I believe that we live in that time in which the Bible said that there would be an outpouring of the Holy Spirit. Some of our "sons and daughters" whom we teach in our Sunday schools have been pre-qualified for the outpouring of the Holy Spirit because they have given their lives to the Lord. What remains is for us to complete the circuit for the power of God to come down to these children.

Take it like this, the function of the switch in any electrical circuit is to complete or disconnect the conducting path. Once you flip the switch, the circuit is completed, and the current will flow to power whatever appliance that you need to power. If you do not flip the switch, the connection will not be made, and power cannot flow. The good news is that if you do not flip the switch, someone else will. If you do not make the vital connection, God will send someone down the road to link the children up with the Holy Spirit. It is a privilege to do so now and let it redound to your eternal credit. One mistake some of us made in the past was to think that we were not qualified to minister the baptism of the Holy Spirit to the children or even to adults. It is possible that while you are reading this, you may be thinking that you are not up to it. You probably think that you need to teach the children for six weeks like we did before they can receive this supernatural experience. Allow me to correct that wrong thinking. Know that you are up to it if you are born again. Ask the Lord for the baptism of the Holy Spirit if you have not yet been baptized. If you are already baptized in the Holy Spirit, you have all that it takes to do the job! You do not have to wait for your pastor or the "prayer warrior" in your church to do it. They may not have the time for the children as you do. It is a matter of simple faith. If you believe that the Lord hears your prayer, go ahead and do it.

Know that it is not you who will baptize the children with

the Holy Ghost. Your role is simply to flip on the switch. The scripture says, "Faith comes by hearing, and hearing, by the word of God" (Romans 10:17). We taught the children for six weeks because we did not know any better. Since then, we do not always go that long before ministering the baptism to the children. One more thing I would like you to note is that if you pray for the children and they do not show any evidence of being baptized, do not get embarrassed or feel any shame that it is because of you. You need to put your faith into action. Believe that the Holy Spirit will come upon them when you pray. Also, note that the individual child needs to express his faith to receive Him. At the confluence of your faith as the one ministering and that of the child comes the miracle.

Therefore, it is important that you directly reference the scriptures in sharing about the person and the ministry of the Holy Spirit. Teach the children that the experience is necessary for their personal walk with the Lord and that it is as real today as it was in the days of Paul and the disciples. When you have fully explained it to them, ask those who want to receive the baptism to indicate their interest. Chances are that all the children in your class will respond positively. Believe them that they are genuine. It is not your responsibility to decide who is genuine or not because you may not know the work the Holy Spirit will do in the heart of a child the moment that you make the call. Go ahead and

207

pray for the children, asking the Lord to fill them with the Holy Spirit and with power. It is good to be prepared before you minister the baptism of the Holy Spirit, but I have not seen in any scripture where it is stipulated that you must fast or have a special way to prepare before you can carry out this function. The only time the Bible talks about fasting before you minister is when you are dealing with some stubborn demons. However, if you schedule a day to pray for the baptism of the Holy Spirit, it is advisable that you bring your body under subjection with fasting and prayer so that you will remain focused on the job at hand without getting distracted.

The Lord taught me this lesson in an interesting way. I had always believed that you need to fast before ministering the baptism in the Holy Spirit until I was invited to a Full Gospel Businessmen's Fellowship International chapter meeting in Port-Harcourt, Nigeria. I had lunch before going to the meeting, not knowing that the chapter president was going to put me on the spot that evening. I was the supervising Field Representative for this chapter of the fellowship. After the message, which was on the baptism in the Holy Spirit, the president made the altar call for those desirous to be baptized. He promptly invited me to pray for them. I did not know if anybody in the fellowship that evening was fasting, but certainly, I was not. To my surprise, when I laid hands on those who responded to the altar call, some of them received the Holy Spirit with the evidence of speaking in tongues. In retrospect, the incident I referred to earlier on, when we went to our regular Happiness Club meeting and saw a classroom full of children, we had not "prepared" in advance to pray for the baptism of the Holy Spirit. We responded to the situation at hand, and God glorified himself. Furthermore, children in our Sunday school ministered to some of their classmates, and they received the baptism. It is good to be spiritually prepared for every Sunday church service, in positive anticipation for anything that may come up—whether it is casting out demons, praying for the sick, or the baptism in the Holy Spirit. We need to be prepared at *every* meeting. It has been our practice for years that we do not eat on Sunday mornings when we are going to minister in one capacity or the other in the church.

When the children get baptized in the Holy Spirit, we have a duty to encourage them to seek the gifts of the Holy Spirit. Again, it is all done in faith. There are several gifts of the Holy Spirit that a child can be blessed with. Let us be mindful of what we teach them about the gifts and their operations. Adults may question your doctrine and do the search for themselves, but more than 90 percent of the children in your class will certainly believe whatever you tell them. It will be unwise and certainly not right to teach the children what cannot be substantiated by the scriptures. Even though it constitutes a doctrine of your church or your pastor's teaching, you must study the scriptures firsthand by yourself and be sure that what you teach the children is scripturally sound. You own whatever you teach and know that you are answerable to God for what you pass on to the children. If you teach the children a wrong doctrine, it does not matter if your church believes it; God will hold you to account. I have attended a meeting where the preacher was teaching people how to string a couple of syllables together and repeat them fast to "speak in tongues." I have also interacted with lovely Christian brothers and sisters whose church denominations do not believe in the baptism of the Holy Spirit. They told me that their church is evangelical but not pentecostal. They believe that the Holy Spirit baptism happened at Pentecost when the Bible records that the disciples of the Lord were in the upper room, and the Holy Spirit came on them like tongues of fire. They contend that the era of the Holy Spirit in the church is over. That is not correct. This kind of doctrine is not scripturally sound. The devil has blinded the eyes of these Christians from knowing the source of power that the Lord has provided us to do the work He has given us to do.

I have also attended a seminar where the speaker was demonstrating to the audience how the Holy Spirit can speak to the children. She said that we should play some soft music and ask the children to close their eyes for a while, and when they open their eyes, we should ask them what they "heard." She then asked the teachers in the audience to close their eyes as she played some soft music. After a few minutes, she asked us to open our eyes. She then asked us what we "heard." Some people in the audience said what they "heard." There was no scriptural foundation for such an activity, and it had every potential to morph into a dangerous practice. Please let us do our part as instructed by scriptures and allow the Holy Spirit to do His. The Holy Spirit can speak to a child in an audible voice. He can whisper into the ears of the children. They do not need soft music as a condition for Him to speak to them. He can speak to them in a crowded restaurant as well as an empty church building or when they are out on a promenade.

The "how to do it" mentality is so pervasive in this digital age that it can steer children into spiritism if we teach them to follow a set of processes and rules. Do not create methods on how the Holy Spirit would give gifts to the children. Would that not be you trying to step into His role? Note that the Bible says that the Holy Spirit distributes the gifts as He pleases. Some may have one gift, and others may have seven or even nine. He knows what each child can handle and what plans He has for each child for kingdom service. Our role is to teach the children sound doctrine. The Bible clearly says,

But the manifestation of the Spirit is given to each one for the profit of all: for to one is given the word of wisdom through the Spirit, to another the word of knowledge through the same spirit, to another, gifts of healings by the same Spirit, to another the working of miracles, to another, prophecy, to another discerning of spirits, to another different kinds of tongues, to another, interpretation of tongues. But one and same Spirit works all these things, distributing to each one as He wills.

1 Corinthians 12:7-11 (NKJV)

Another error we may be tempted to make is to assume that we know the age that a child can receive the baptism in the Holy Spirit. Nothing can be further from the truth. We do not know. Please do not put a lid on this supernatural experience for your pupils. One of the teachers in our children's department shared with me recently that her child got born again at three and filled with the Holy Spirit at age six. The child is a grown adult and has been following the Lord ever since and serving in His vineyard. Give the Holy Spirit His rightful seat in your children's ministry and see what He will do with you.

10

Safety Issues

Their peace, comfort, and joy are our priorities

It is a supreme act of trust for a parent to drop off his child and entrust him to our care in the children's ministry. Every parent who drops off a child in our children's Sunday school does so from a default faith premise that the child will be safe, and there are adults in the children's church or Sunday school who place a premium on the physical, psychological, and spiritual safety of the child.

Where else could a child be safer than in the house of God? Unfortunately, a shadow has been cast on this trust.

213

Sex scandals associated with priests in the Catholic and other churches in recent years, making national headlines, have blatantly betrayed such trust. Sadly, other organizations such as the Boys' Scouts of America also identified leaders who abused the privilege of taking care of children entrusted to them by unsuspecting parents. Such revelations are not only shocking and sad but are a mortifying shame, especially where the house of God and the practice of faith are involved. The betrayal and descent to abysmally low levels of irreverence expose an absence of fear of God and reveal an irreverent familiarity with His work. The perpetrators are brazen, and not only did they desecrate a place of holiness and unbridled righteousness, but they further went on in vile impunity to destroy the lives of innocent children—*in the house of God.*

These reported heartbreaking occurrences call for an urgent rethink and reordering of priorities and structures. It is our responsibility to put structures in place in our children's ministries to ensure that the children's Sunday school is decidedly safe for every child in our care.

Let us briefly examine different areas where safety can be compromised in our children's Sunday school departments.

Active shooter in church

On June 15, 2017, normal programming on most news outlets in the United States was interrupted with the breaking news that a self-styled white supremacist shot and killed nine African Americans in Charleston, South Carolina, during a Bible study at the Emmanuel African Methodist Episcopal Church (AME). That attack in the hallowed place of worship seems to have emboldened more copycat shooters to target vulnerable places of worship in recent years. A gunman opened fire on parishioners who were worshipping in West Freeway Church of Christ in Texas, killing one person before he was killed by an armed member of the congregation. Church and synagogue shootings, just like school shootings, have become a serious security concern in the United States of America, and several churches have put in place contingency plans to avoid mass casualties should such occur in their churches.

It is an unfortunate development in the American society that budgets for evangelism are now being diverted to security matters, but that is the reality that churches must grapple with in this age. It is our responsibility as children's church teachers to work with the leadership team of our churches and come up with contingency plans for protecting our pupils should such an unfortunate situation arise. Most churches have security departments that look out for the protection

215

of worshippers and property of the church during church services. If your church does not have such departments in place, it would be wise to suggest to the leadership team that this issue be addressed within the shortest time possible.

Kidnapping from church

Kidnapping in schools and churches has become a common concern that needs to be addressed by the appropriate authorities. The church should be the last place anybody in his right mind should think of when planning to commit a crime. However, it has become a major target for children abductors. There are two types of kidnappers that are involved in the kidnapping of children from the church. Parent kidnappers seem to be more common than strangers. Parent kidnapping of children, especially in the United States, occurs when one of the parents who does not have a custodial right kidnaps his or her child. It sounds absurd to think of a parent kidnapping his child. However, the justice system recognizes that a parent who, by his actions: criminal activities and associations, or exposure to substances and situations that may harm a child, is not allowed custody of the child. In divorce cases, the court awards the primary custody of a child to one of the parents and gives a visitation right at given times (like every other weekend) to the other. Except where explicitly indicated, most teachers may not be aware of these family dynamics.

Consider a scenario where Casey drops off her seven-year-old son Bobby in the children's Sunday school and goes for worship in the sanctuary. Her ex-husband comes during the service and goes straight to the children's department and asks his son's teacher to release the boy because he needs to go to work. The teacher obliges. He has seen George drop off Bobby several times in the past and knows that he is Bobby's father. By the close of service, Casey comes over to the children's department to pick up Bobby only to discover that George, her ex-husband, has pulled a fast one on her by violating the custodial rights ordered by the divorce court. This is a common scenario that plays out in most cases of children being kidnapped in the church by their parents. Often, an amber alert is not issued because the police may not have sufficient reasons to believe that the child is in any imminent danger. Depending on where they live, George and Bobby may well be in another state or perhaps another country before anybody realizes that a crime has been committed. However, by accepting Bobby into the children's church, the church assumed temporary custodial responsibility for the child and is legally responsible for whatever happens to Bobby. That is one of the reasons the children's department needs to have clear-cut policies on the procedures for accepting and releasing children from their family members or anybody. Divorce can be messy, and children's Sunday school teachers should not be unwitting accessories to its gory chessboard maneuvers.

The second group of kidnappers is complete strangers who have criminal intents in settling scores, making money, or satisfying a deranged psychological craving. A story published online in June 2009 by the Grand Rapids Press[5] describes a bizarre situation in which a volunteer in a children's department kidnapped one of the children in the church. However, the diligence of the church by having safety protocols in place, including security cameras, saved the day. Below is the account by Lori Niedenfuer Cool with contributions by Press reporter John Tunison.

Savannah Nolf, who turns 1 on Friday, and her dad, Tom Nolf. Savannah was kidnapped from church daycare on Sunday.

Jessie and Tom Nolf were just glad to have their little girl, who turns 1 on Friday, back home. They left her in the nursery while they attended the 11 a.m. service at the Kentwood church, 1200 60th St. SE. During the service, church officials summoned the parents and said they could not find the girl. They asked what Savannah was wearing, and searched rooms near the nursery. As time went on, the parents become increasingly concerned. Initially, they believed she would turn up quickly. "At the same time, in the back of my mind, I'm saying, 'OK, what's going on?" the father said. "Where's my kid? ... Is my kid going to end up on the back of a milk carton?" Police used surveillance video taken inside the church and identified Reid, who is a registered volunteer. Police issued an area broadcast alerting other agencies that a young woman wearing a sundress, holding a baby in a red dress, was spotted leaving the church. Sheriff's Deputy Todd Summerhays heard the notice and recalled seeing a woman matching that description earlier that day walking on 68th Street in the Cutlerville area. Police went to Reid's home, and found Reid holding the girl, who was unharmed. During police interviews, Reid told detectives that she put a daughter, named Savannah, up for adoption two years ago. Later, she told police she made up that story, and told investigators that she "always wanted to be a mother, which (led) her to take the child," Detective Jason Richards wrote in an arrest affidavit.

She told police she did not know the child or her parents before taking her, Richards wrote. "She was caring for the child within the nursery program at Kentwood Community Church, saw Savannah and decided to take her from the church and admitted to taking her back to her residence ... where she was subsequently arrested," the detective wrote. Savannah's parents can't make sense of the abduction. "We still have no idea what was going through (Reid's) mind," Tom Nolf said. "It was just crazy—it's all surreal. I'm still in shock." He said Reid had put his daughter's hair up, changed her clothes, and told police the girl belonged to her. Nolf said he didn't blame the church, which had a security plan in place, but didn't know if his family would return. It was only their second visit. Reid has volunteered at the church since she was 12 and had passed background checks. "I guess she just snapped," Nolf said. We're so thankful to God. I know it's not always (a good ending). It had to be on Father's Day, of all days.

(all grammar and spelling has been left unedited)

This story illustrates the reality of the problem that a children's department of a church can face no matter whom we have on staff. In this case, the lady (Reid) had been volunteering in the nursery since she was twelve years old and had passed background checks. There was nothing in her record that suggested that she had criminal tendencies, yet she abducted a child because she had always wanted to be a mother. Thank God the child was not harmed. In some cases, the story does not end well.

Teachers should endeavor to get as much information about the children in their care as possible. Getting to know the family a bit may help identify red flags when they pop up. One thing the church did right in this story is that it had a security plan in place, which was activated as soon as someone noticed that the child was missing. Time was of the essence. Reid did not have sufficient time to execute another plan (if she had any) before she was arrested, and the child was retrieved. Security cameras are gadgets that we pay heavily for but pray that we would not have any reasons to use them. Still, in the moment of anxiety, they can be helpful resources. Nevertheless, no matter how careful we are, let us remember that "We do not wrestle against flesh and blood but against principalities, against powers, against the rulers of the darkness of this age, against spiritual hosts of wickedness in heavenly places" (Ephesians 6:12, NKJV). The hosts of darkness stand ready any day to embarrass us and

221

put the church in legal, financial, and moral jeopardy. The need to pray for the children's ministry is crucial and cannot be downplayed. Here is a family visiting the church for the second time. They had not settled down to get to know the flavor and spiritual tone of the church before the devil struck. No matter what anyone says about the church, this one family had a bad taste that will linger in their consciousness for a long time, and the abducted child might have to deal with the trauma for years.

In my years of service in the children's ministry, I have had two major scares. In the first instance, I was the coordinator of the children's ministry, and we had a situation where one of the children slipped out of the class and was found alone in the parking lot playing by himself. His class teacher did not notice that he was not in the class until a church member saw him and brought him back to the children's department. The church was in a quiet residential neighborhood in the outskirts of the city, with acres of vacant land between it and the next building. He was potentially easy prey for any criminal adventure. After that experience, we took extra measures to secure the children's church. The outer door was changed to a heavier and safer door and bathroom times for the pupils were better supervised and regulated. The second experience was at a regular children's Sunday service. I noticed that the sibling of one of the children in my class was not present and still did not show up after some time. I asked her brother why she did not come to church, and he told me that she *was* in church. A red flag immediately popped up in my mind! She did not loathe children's Sunday school, so truancy was canceled out. On the contrary, she loved the class lessons and used to participate actively. To be in church and not come to class, what was going on? Her brother had no clue as to her whereabouts. I felt that something was wrong and cut short my teaching; I hurried to the sanctuary and had the ushers call out her mother. Being a worker in the church, the mother oftentimes allowed her children to check themselves into the children's department. When she affirmed that the twelve-year-old and her brother came down to my class together, yet she was not in class, we knew that we had a problem on our hands. My mind raced through a few scenarios. Her mother, understandably, was becoming agitated. We both began a frantic search. We checked in the parking lot, the youth class, the sanctuary—everywhere and anywhere but still did not find her. Her mother went to check the car. No, she was not there. Wondering what might have happened, I had to go back to my class while her mother continued the search. Lo and behold! I bumped into her in the hallway, looking uncharacteristically sullen. She told me that she was "having a bad day" and wanted to be alone. She had chosen one of the ladies' restrooms as her interim place of solitude. Was I relieved that we "found" her! The negative thoughts of disaster that pulled me from all directions never happened. Thank God! These were two very scary moments of my Sunday school teaching experience. I am grateful not to have had many scary situations and thankful that the two I had ended well.

However, each incident impressed upon me the priority importance for the children's department to work in sync with the church leadership so as to ensure that security plans and measures guaranteeing the safety of our charges were put in place.

Medical emergencies

Some medical emergencies may develop while a child is in our care. Each children's department should have a protocol in place and a process for alerting parents when there is a medical emergency. In some churches, each class teacher has the parent's cell phone number and can reach them directly. In others, a child's check-in ID number or the parent's cell phone number is projected on the screen in the sanctuary to alert the parents of a situation that requires their immediate attention. Allergies are usually the number one medical emergency that children suffer. Some children's departments have identification cards that the children wear, and their allergies are written on these cards for the teachers and their assistants to take note of. Some parents may not want their children's allergies displayed for other children or individuals not directly involved in their care to be privy to. Whatever the department's policies, it would be useful to work with parents and respect their sensitivities to their child's personal medical issues. It may help to design general medical information forms that parents must complete and provide information about health concerns that their child's teacher should be aware of but keep confidential. In case of a life-threatening emergency, the teacher should call 911 and then alert the parents or guardians of the child.

Seizures are also potential medical emergencies for kids. When a child in your care is having a seizure, do not raise the alarm. If you are trained in first aid, follow the laid down procedures for handling seizures. Take charge and ensure that the other children do not crowd around him. If you are not trained, call any teacher who has such training to take over while you take away the other children from the environment. Ask someone to contact the child's parents. Ideally, every teacher in the children's department should be certified in first aid and CPR techniques. If there are no teachers trained in first aid, call 911 immediately and let the parents know.

Children cherish playtime a lot and look forward to it. However, accidents do occur during playtime. Each children's department should have a first aid box that teachers could use if an accident happens and the injuries are mild. Parents should be notified as soon as possible. If the injury is

225

life-threatening, please call 911 and let the parents know as soon as possible. I am thankful to the Lord that in nearly fifty years of teaching in children's Sunday school, I have not had to deal with a major medical emergency, although I have a certification in first aid and CPR, and I am a pharmacist. Once, we had a case of nosebleeds, but the class teachers were up to it. Two of them are nurses, and they handled the situation appropriately.

Safe teachers and handlers

Following the sex scandals associated with some catholic priests and other church leaders, the problem of sexual abuse and molestation of children has become an open wound in recent times. It is heart-breaking to hear of individuals charged with taking care of children turning around to steal their innocence and trust, exposing them to a life of psychological trauma. We must be observant, watchful, sensitive, and committed to protect the innocence of our charges and guard against any ills that can directly pose an exposure to mental, psychological, and physical trauma. Unfortunately, victims of child abuse often recoil and suffer in silence, many believing themselves responsible for their misfortune. Thus, every children's department needs to put in place a policy defining who is qualified to teach or volunteer to help in the children's department. Background checks are excellent ways of digging into the past of teachers. I must confess that I was deeply conflicted with this for years, and here is why. I believe that "If the Son makes you free, you are free indeed." If so, are we saying that a person who is now born-again cannot teach children because of his sordid past? This thought burdened me for years as I handled questions on background checks for teachers. However, I have concluded that the background checks help the teacher not to fall into any besetting sin that will take him back to his old ways. I have come to view the situation in the following light: if a man was an alcoholic prior to surrendering his life to the Lord, the worst place for him to get employment is in a bar. The temptation could be overwhelming for him. In the same way, if a potential teacher is known to abuse children, it is for his own spiritual good to be involved in other ministries like the choir or the technical department than teaching in the children's Sunday school.

Every teacher needs to have a security clearance to be eligible to teach in the children's department. What we need is the consent of the teachers to do the background check. I would encourage the church administration to take the financial burden off the teachers. I appreciate that the pressure to find persons to care for the children is enormous. It may be tempting to look the other way if people with an uncomfortable past present themselves to teach in Sunday school. However, the risk and possible consequences are too weighty to allow a compromised acceptance. Both for the children's sake and the would-be teachers, the church authority must take a firm stand, *albeit* in the spirit of love. It would be advisable to follow a rejected application with a Holy Spirit-guided and prayerful conversation with the individual.

Another group of teachers may not have any untoward character failure gleaned from background checks of their past, but in the course of interacting with and teaching the children, it may be observed that they develop what the Bible calls an "inordinate affection" towards the children. This may be deleterious to the upbringing of the children, and it behooves other teachers to call out such a person privately and firmly present him/her with the concern, but in a spirit of love, to render him/her accountable. We must be vigilant and be our brother's keeper. For better control and management, as well as to provide the necessary checks and balances, I strongly recommend the children's church or church leadership to ensure that there are two teachers in each class; and that teachers should avoid being alone with any child in their charge. The older the children, the greater the need to exercise more care in dealing with them. If a teacher behaves inappropriately towards a child, we should exercise sound judgment and report to the supervising authorities to decide what penalty the behavior merits: a warning or complete removal from the children's ministry. The flock of lambs the

Lord has put in our care must be jealously guarded.

Check-in and tracking

The safety and spiritual environment of a child are the two major issues that parents visiting our churches for the first time look out for. We need to encourage them to have confidence in our system by the way we set up and run our check-in and check-out processes. The old-fashioned name tag is one of the cheap and effective ways to keep children safe in our Sunday schools. During check-in, a child is given a tag with an identification number, and a matching tag is given to the parent or guardian. The child should not be released to any other person without the matching tag. This is especially necessary for large churches but is no less important in smaller churches. There are different types of tags that can be used. There are disposable tags and permanent tags. The disposable tags are issued every Sunday, but the permanent ones are given once and could be laminated for durability. The family's identification or authorized cell phone number is clearly printed on both tags. Each family has the responsibility of bringing the tags to church. Also, it is the family's responsibility to ensure that the authorized individual has the tag during check-ins and check-outs.

Technology-based check-in systems are becoming more

popular in churches in the United States, and there are different companies that offer a variety of products ranging in price from about a few hundreds to thousands of dollars. Some of the products are web-based. A family can register or check in their children online. Alternatively, the family checks in children in church with an iPad or a computer using a software-based system. The check-in process can be self-directed or handled by a trained volunteer. Computer stations or kiosks are conveniently located either at the foyer of the church building, the entrance to the children's department, or any easily accessible room or space clearly designated for it. The number of check-in stations your church needs will depend on the population of the children in the church and what type of check-in process and software that you are using.

For children ministries that are considering web-based or software-based check-in systems, it is advisable to consider the cost, the population of children in the church, computer literacy levels of the parents who attend the church, and whether the service is subscription-based or one-time purchase offer. Other things to consider are whether the package includes training for all the volunteers in your children's Sunday school or just one volunteer, the maintenance of the platform, upgrades of the software you are interested in (if you plan to use a software-based platform, you may need to purchase new software to stay current with upgrades). If you are considering self-directed check-ins where the parents do it on their own, it is advisable to go for a user-friendly system that does not require multiple steps. Most parents struggle every Sunday morning to get their children ready for church service, and many are not likely to get to church earlier than ten minutes to the beginning of service. If they must check their children in, they will need to accomplish that in less than five minutes. A check-in system that takes longer than five minutes to complete may create a backup that will frustrate parents. The children's Sunday school leadership should work with the technical department of the church to select a functional and affordable system that will make it easy for parents and teachers to check in the children without hassles on a Sunday morning. The opinions of teachers and parents who are the end-users of this technology should be accommodated in the final choice of the system that will work for your church.

11

TEEM-ED Model of Children's Ministry

A paradigm shift but the same message

Is Sunday school dead? Some believe that the Sunday school model, which was introduced in the 1800s, has not evolved much despite all the cultural shifts and advancements in technology. One staggering fact that we cannot overlook is that most churches are experiencing a rapid decline in the attendance to children's Sunday school, and worse still, the quality of the products of many Sunday schools leave much to be desired. As stated earlier, the children going through our Sunday schools are mainly exposed to cultural Christianity rather than committed Christianity, and when they have the opportunity to leave home, independent of parental controls, they veer towards the new age religion or no religion at all. It is in this context that several voices have arisen in recent times calling for a paradigm shift towards a creative, Christ-centered, and appealing model that incorporates digital resources and methods in the delivery of our messages to the children. A couple of online models have emerged that are targeted at helping churches and children's ministries optimize their Sunday school systems to fully engage the children in a participatory Sunday school experience. One thread that runs through all the models is the goal to provide focused Bible-based programs that will ensure that our children are steeped in committed Christianity by the time they graduate into young adult classes.

To the glory of God, the children's ministries that I have been privileged to participate in have been effective in producing graduates who continue as committed Christians even as adults. In making these claims, I am aware that it is the Lord who knows the heart of everyone. However, going by what we see, the zeal and commitment in serving the Lord, more than 90 percent of the children we have trained over these many years are active in the household of God. We have developed an integrated program that incorporates elements of our practices that some of the children we trained say helped their continued Christian growth. Our model is called the TEEM-ED model. The term TEEM-ED is an acronym for Train, Evangelize, Equip, Mentor, Empower and Develop.

The approach to children's ministry which we have developed dates back to the 1970s when we were undergraduate students at the University of Ife in Nigeria. Our chapel in the university was run by the mainstream traditional protestant churches, including the Anglican, Methodist, Presbyterian, and Baptist denominations. The mode of worship for the earlier part of my stay in the university was cool traditional liturgies. Nothing loud, no gospel band, and no speaking in tongues. We sang hymns, followed prayers from the prayer books, and listened to sermons, most of which I would characterize as philosophical and motivational speeches that seemed to glorify the preacher more than they glorified Christ. Students and staff attended church services on Sunday mornings more like rituals that were not aggressive in seeking for a change in their sinful life practices. Contrast that with the loud Evangelical Christian Union (ECU) evening fellowship meetings at the same chapel venue that held from four o'clock.

The ECU was an aggressive, result-oriented Pentecostal fellowship where most of us cut our spiritual teeth in a more liberal college environment. We were grounded in the scriptures through a systematic weekly Bible study organized by the fellowship. Sunday evenings were such glorious super-natural encounters. Our worship was way out of this world, and prayer sessions were filled with the Elijah-type, right-on-the-mark prophecies. There was hardly any Sunday that we would not hear directly from God by prophecy. We were taught to follow the scriptures "precept upon precept, line upon line." Throw into that mix the rare privilege of having Pastor S.G Elton, who visited our fellowship and ministered to us frequently. Pastor Elton was a British missionary who resigned his job as a British Broadcasting Corporation (BBC) engineer in 1933 to answer God's call to serve in Nigeria. He was arguably the father of Pentecostal Christianity in Nigeria. His mission field was primarily the colleges and universities in Nigeria. He lived in a city called Ilesha, which was about a ten to fifteen minutes drive from our campus. Although he traveled quite a bit, visiting university campuses all over Nigeria, the proximity of our campus to his residence gave us the privilege of having him visit our fellowship more frequently than he visited the others. We could also pop into his home as often as we wanted. We were like his children. He diligently taught us and manifested several gifts of the Holy Spirit during our meetings. His messages were loaded with prophecies, words of knowledge, and words of wisdom.

The ECU, under his watchful apostolic eyes, organized

a campus-wide open-air meeting on April 20, 1973, during which the power of God enveloped the university campus. Students from the fellowship preached and prayed. The blind saw, and the lame walked, and a dumb man spoke. That was the type of fellowship that produced the children's Sunday school teachers that I met when I joined the church in 1974 and continued to provide that service to the chapel until we left the university in 1990. With that kind of background, we had teachers who dedicated themselves to teaching the children the undiluted word of God. However, something was missing. I did not see these highly spiritual teachers teach the children about the Holy Spirit. Neither did I. I do not know if they were going through similar rationalizations as I was having those days. I did not want to upset the traditional order of the mainstream chapel. Also, I wondered if children that young would be able to handle the subject of the Holy Spirit. All that changed in 1985-1986 when we had the mighty outpouring of the Holy Spirit on the children in our Sunday school and Happiness Club.

As our ministry gradually evolved, one of the teachers in our Sunday school called Obiora Nwosu told us that the Lord spoke to him one morning and asked him to start a children's club for Him. He got some children together and taught them to beat the drum. Then he shared the vision with our children's Sunday school secretary, Nath Nwanpka, who at that time was a graduate student studying for his PhD in education. Nath invited me to teach the children some drama and songs. Obiora named the group Happiness Club. The year was 1980, and I had just started my master's degree program. By the end of the academic year, both Nath and Obiora completed their programs and left the university. The mantle fell on me to nurture the young activity group. As we poured ourselves into it, the Lord opened doors, and before long, we were ministering to audiences in an annual national music concert called Livingspring. We were on national television and were also invited to minister at the National Theatre. The group gained wide national recognition, and we traveled quite a bit. Traveling became an integral component of our children's ministry. In later years, some of the children that we raised for the Lord told me that the traveling part made a huge impact on their growing-up years. We have retained traveling in the form of field trips or ministration outreaches as one of the pillars of our program. Our songs were original. Some of our pupils who eventually went to secondary schools outside Ife had dozens of original compositions they learned in Happiness Club to share with other students in their schools. Some of them became their school's choir leaders, while others played in their school's band.

It became clear to us that our role was to provide the children with an enabling and friendly environment where their talents would be discovered, developed, and deployed to the service of the Lord. Integrating this with an uncompromising, undiluted teaching of the Word of God led to the development of the TEEM-ED model.

Train

In the TEEM-ED Model of children's ministry, we emphasize training rather than teaching as an effective way of bringing up the children in our care. We are intentional and focused on choosing what to share with the children and how to do it. We use a variety of techniques and methods to emphasize our object lesson. For example, it is not enough to teach the children about Noah's Ark, ask them questions, and give them prizes. In the TEEM-ED model, that is the beginning of the immersion process. We shall dive in a little deeper. The fastest animals like the cheetah were in Noah's Ark, so were the slow-moving animals like the snail and the tortoise. Noah could have closed the door of the Ark when the cheetahs of this world made it to their safe haven, but he waited for the snails and tortoises to crawl into the big boat. We would make the children think through the importance of having such a large family of believers, each person with his experience, motivation, and foibles in the household of God. How about Noah building a ship on dry land? He did not have any technology to haul the big sea-going vessel from the construction site to the sea. The whole idea sounds crazy, and for good measure, cynics in Noah's time must have considered him in need of a psychiatrist. His implicit obedience to the voice of God was unparalleled in his time. In the end, he had the last laugh. How would that relate to contemporary Christianity? We ask the children to think through these issues and come up with insights for the class to learn from. Over the years and in different churches, the insights we get from the children have been mind-blowing. This approach helps the children develop their critical thinking skills and gets them to participate in the lessons, not as docile consumers of the information that we pass down to them but also as active creators of knowledge. They feel accomplished whenever I select their insights for the entire class to listen to. Part of what we do to motivate the children is to select the three most thoughtful insights and share them with the entire class. Occasionally, we would have the class write down in their notebooks the best insight for the day. It is amazing how other children would endeavor to have their own insights recognized in subsequent class sessions. The healthy competition creates an atmosphere of quality productivity as each child works hard to showcase his ability. Often, there are a few that dominate the top positions on a regular basis. We do not deny them the opportunity to be recognized. We showcase them as the standard-bearers and allow the other children to come up to their level rather than lower the standards.

Still using the story of Noah as an illustration, the next stage is to give the children a comprehension exercise and grade their papers. We will follow it up by asking a child to summarize the passage. The teacher will then present the lesson for the day. The main insight from either the pupils' contribution or the teacher's lesson will form the subject on which the children would develop a skit or song. The training does not end with the classwork. The children are given memory verses to work on and present to the class. In all, the immersion program trains the child to be proficient in the Word—both in the letter and the spirit.

Evangelize

Our primary goal is to lead a child to Christ. We also need to intentionally develop plans to sustain his interest in remaining a Christian. This is quite a heavy lift as we do not know exactly where each child stands in his walk with the Lord. However, we can create an enabling environment that will encourage the child to live a Christian life happily. To begin with, the children look up to us and see us as the representatives of the Lord Jesus Christ. They would like to emulate us most of the time. Whatever character we display to the children in our care will either bring them closer to Christ or repel them from Him. You are the best specimen of Christianity that the child sees. Does what he sees encourage him to become and continue on the path he has chosen, or does he look for something else? We are more effective as teachers when we model quality Christian behavior and character to the children. For some of the children who are not yet born again, we will win them to Christ by the fruits of our lives that they see. In his book *The 21 Irrefutable Laws of Leadership*[6], John Maxwell writes about the law of the picture in which he encourages leaders to model their vision to those that they lead. According to him, "The leader's modeling of the vision makes the picture come alive." Children process information differently from adults. The less abstract the information, the more comprehensible it is to them. Salvation may be an abstract concept, but the picture of a saved person that they see is you. If they see genuine love and kindness, they will respond to it positively. On the other hand, if all they see is someone trying to do a duty but does not have the character to sell the abstract concept of salvation, they will not be interested. The TEEM-ED model places emphasis on leading a child to the Lord. We encourage teachers to use the wordless book, songs, skits, class presentations, movies, or direct messages to bring the child to the Lord. Every teacher is encouraged to make the altar call as frequently as possible in the children's Sunday school until you are sure that all the children in your class have genuinely committed their lives to the Lord. It may sound monotonous, but you never know when a child will be ready. I remember the story my wife shared with us about how she gave her life to the Lord.

She was a freshman on the campus of the University of Ife in Nigeria when she surrendered to the Lord. She attended a campus-wide open-air meeting (crusade) during which the world-renowned preacher Benson Idahosa preached. The first night, the preacher painted a picture of what eternity without the Lord meant. Vickie did not answer the altar call that night. When the altar call ended, she felt like the door of heaven had been shut against her. So, she cried as she ran all the way back to her dorm. What if she died that night? She was sure that she would not go to heaven. She said that she prayed hard that night, asking the Lord to spare her life till the next meeting. During the second night of the crusade, she said that it did not matter what the preacher preached about; all that she waited for was the altar call. As soon as the preacher made the altar call, she was among the first to respond. What if the preacher did not make the altar call that night? The point here is that the TEEM-ED model considers frequent altar calls at our regular meetings a necessity. Create the opportunity and let the Holy Spirit do His work in the lives of the children.

Equip

The whole idea of a school is to create a learning environment where the students are provided with the tools that equip them to pursue a career, learn a trade, or simply develop themselves to be better members of society. One of our goals in the TEEM-ED program is to provide our pupils with information and tools that equip them to live committed Christian lives. We encourage a systematic and goal-oriented Bible study program that maps out the course the children will take at every level of their stay in the children's Sunday school. It is an integrated approach that creates a course sequence in which there are prerequisites and corequisites in the design of our curricula. For example, we can spend the earlier years telling the Bible stories and teaching the children about Bible characters but spend their capstone year studying Bible principles and doctrines. We also encourage the children to have practical experiences with developing a personal walk with the Lord through a consistent quiet time and a personal Bible study program. We challenge them to memorize as many scriptures as possible. The TEEM-ED approach to children's ministry is big on worship, memory verse challenges, and baptism in the Holy Spirit. These are the tools that will help them grow into the fullness of Christ and live for Him in the future. They are also trained to share the word with other people.

Mentor

Mentoring is an informal relationship in which someone with more experience or expertise (mentor) transmits knowledge or information to a younger or less experienced person (mentee). It is a quasi-apprenticeship situation in which the mentor trains, advises, or provides expert support to a mentee. Our children ministries are filled with children who are looking for directions in life. Some come from dysfunctional homes where parents are at daggers drawn with each other. All they know is the language of violence and privations. They loathe going home for fear of what they will meet on any given day. They hate holidays like Christmas and Thanksgiving because the worst comes out of the adults in their lives during these otherwise great occasions. If you look around in your Sunday school class, you can easily identify them. They are looking for trustworthy adults in their lives. They are looking for a substitute parent and guide. We are privileged to be available to play that role. Even if a child comes from a well-to-do family, there are still areas where he needs a mentor. One of the children in my class came from what people would consider a dream family. His parents were well-educated Christians, and both were in the medical profession. Still, I had a role to play in his life. I remember drumming it into him that he was such a smart boy, and I would like to see him go for the Ivy League schools. I constantly reminded him that he needed to work towards that goal. He did. Today he is in one of the best ivy league universities in the United States. Beyond his academics, I also found a niche in being part of his spiritual development. I challenged him to memorize the scriptures and develop a personal relationship with God. He is among the children that graduated from our program who could recite more than one hundred verses of the scriptures conveniently. We also worked with him to develop short sermons and gave him the opportunity to present them during our ministrations either in our church or whenever we were invited to some programs in other churches or ministries. By age ten, he was preaching sermons like a seasoned preacher.

On the other hand, we had children in our Sunday school classes who literally grew up in what I refer to as *battle-ground families*. Without being unduly nosy or intrusive, we provided them shoulders to cry on and pointed them to the way they ought to go in life. We were there for them, and when I look back and see the gems that they have become despite the turbulent environments that they grew up in, I thank the Lord that we were available to offer guidance and advice that helped them navigate the adverse realities of their existence. Our mentoring did not stop at the Sunday school. We still mentor many of the children that went through our programs up till today. Many of them have gone on to respectable professions and ministries but still call on us from time to time when they have issues that they need godly counsel on. The TEEM-ED model of children's ministry encourages teachers to be mentors to our pupils. The joy of seeing a life you gave a helping hand blossom right before your eyes is priceless. We pray that the Lord will help us to live the godly lives that will encourage our mentees to do the same.

Empower

For most of the three years that the Lord Jesus carried out His ministry on earth, His disciples were mere witnesses to the miracles that He performed. They were there when He cleansed the leper. They watched Him heal the noble man's son, turn water into wine at the wedding in Cana in Galilee, cast out demons from the demoniacs, heal Peter's mother-in-law, the paralytic who was lowered down from the roof by his friends, and the centurion's servant. I guess that they watched in utter amazement when He raised the widow's son, the ruler's daughter, and Lazarus from the dead. They were present when he performed the many miracles that he did, but not even one of them requested to perform one miracle except when Peter asked if he could also walk on water. However, being the great leader that He was, He decided to transfer power and authority to His disciples and by extension to all who believed in Him thereafter. The disciples had spent all these years observing Him perform the miracles, but there is a great difference between observing and doing something. They needed a practical session. They needed hands-on experience, and that is why Jesus sent them out to preach and demonstrate the power of God. He commissioned them to do all the things that He was doing according to the scriptures.

> And when He had called His twelve disciples to Him, He gave them power over unclean spirits, to cast them out, and to heal all kinds of sickness and all kinds of disease...These twelve Jesus sent out and commanded them, saying: 'Do not go into the way of the Gentiles, and do not enter a city of the Samaritans. But go rather to the lost sheep of the house of Israel. And as you go, preach, saying, The kingdom of heaven is at hand. Heal the sick, cleanse the lepers, raise the dead, cast out demons. Freely you have received, freely give.'

Matthew 10:1, 5-8 (NKJV)

Being empowered by the one whom they had seen command the storm to cease, and it happened exactly as He said, must have been reassuring. They had seen Him do it, but now He tells them that they could do the same things He did all in His name. It was like giving them the staff of the office or the key to the seat of power.

In another instant, he sent out seventy of his disciples into the mission field to gain practical experience in evangelism.

> After these things the Lord appointed seventy others also, and sent them two by two before His face into every city and place where He Himself was about to go. Then He said to them, "The harvest truly is great, but the laborers are few; therefore pray the Lord of the harvest to send out laborers into His harvest. Go your way; behold, I send you out as lambs among wolves.
>
> Luke 10:1-3 (NKJV)

Notice how excited they were when they came back to file their reports: "Then the seventy returned with joy, saying, 'Lord, even the demons are subject to us in Your name'" (Luke 10:17, NKJV).

Following this example of our Lord Jesus Christ, the TEEM-ED model is designed to prepare the children for ministry and create opportunities for them to go out and minister. The preparation starts with the processes described above. The children who give their lives to the Lord Jesus Christ are encouraged to be baptized in the Holy Spirit and seek the gifts of the Holy Spirit. They are encouraged to share the gospel message with their friends, classmates, and family. They are also trained to preach. We make the children conscious of the fact that every Christian is a minister of the gospel. Everyone does not have to be a pastor or an Evangelist to be able to share the gospel message with whoever the Lord leads them to minister to. The practices which we have from time to time diminish stage fright, prepare the children to make presentations publicly, and pray prayers that get results. They also inoculate the children from any fear when they deal with demons. Even adults get frightened when demons manifest, but we train the children to know that all power in heaven and on earth is given to the Lord Jesus Christ, whom they represent. They are trained to remember that according to the scriptures, greater is He who is in them than he who is in the world, and at the name of Jesus Christ, every knee must bow. We teach them to know that they are seated in heavenly places with the Lord Jesus Christ, far above principalities and powers. Orders issue from top to bottom and not the other way round. Since the children are above the principalities and powers, the devils must obey them when they speak in the name of Jesus. It is a settled law. It cannot be otherwise. With their faith fired up, some of our pupils have confronted demons and cast them out from other children. They prayed for the sick, and they recovered. They have also preached the gospel boldly in different settings. We have taken them to churches and Christian programs where they have ministered, knowing that they were not just entertaining but ministering to the souls of men, women, boys, and girls. The children who go through our programs are immersed in the scriptures and encouraged to walk in the supernatural.

Walking in the supernatural without love is a useless activity. Consequently, the TEEM-ED model of children's ministry encourages activities that promote love, respect, and collegiality among the children that we take care of. When we were living in Maryland, children in our junior classes in Bethel Fellowship Church in Glendale had a special program called Sleepover Nights with Auntie Stella. It was an informal program organized by one of our children's Sunday school teachers—Auntie Stella Onuoha. With the permission of their parents, the children spent some weekends with the teacher. It was a time of bonding and developing relationships. Now that the children in that cohort are in their twenties, I see the friendship that they developed in those days blossom into something of beauty. I believe that some are on track to becoming life-long friendships.

Develop

I had a nasty experience with one of my former Sunday school pupils that changed my entire approach to ministering to children. He was one of our pupils in the late seventies. He was a tall, handsome, soft-spoken, and extremely talented kid. While he was in our children's Sunday school, Mike (not his real name) was the kind of child that you would hardly hear his voice when others were chattering. He was a perfect gentleman, obedient and conscientious. He graduated from our Sunday school years before we started Happiness Club in 1980. In fact, by 1980, he was enrolled in the same university, studying for his undergraduate degree.

We had permission from the principal of the University Staff School to use its assembly hall every Saturday from 4 p.m. to 6 p.m. for our Happiness Club sessions. When we got to the school premises on this day, Mike (now an undergraduate student in the university) was having a rehearsal on the stage with a rock band which he seemed to be leading. I approached him to let him know that it was time for our practice. The way he snapped back at me with words I cannot repeat here shocked me. What went wrong? How did this sweet, gentle soul turn into a tiger? What happened to all that we taught him in the children's Sunday school? Where did we get it wrong? Although we got the issue resolved that day, his outburst really got me thinking. Something was wrong with what we were doing as teachers. The boy was quite talented in playing musical instruments, but there was nobody to channel his talent into godly purposes. Mike joined (or probably started) a rock band to give full expression to his musical talents. Unfortunately, that drove him further away from the Lord. I was not hearing Mike yell at me that day. It was not the sweet boy I knew. Something in him could not stand the presence of God that invaded his space that evening. Later, we made Mike our prayer project. I have not seen him ever since, but I am told that he came back to the Lord fully.

After that encounter, it became clear to me that a major plank on which our approach to children's ministry rested was to discover and develop the talents of the children and create opportunities to channel them to the service of the Lord. That has been our focus and approach from 1980 till now. We have made the development of the children's talents one of the central tenets of our TEEM-ED model of children's ministry. I believe that every child has a talent that can be developed and channeled to the service of the Lord. Some are gifted in singing but need some voice training to bring out the gem in them. Others are gifted in acting, public speaking, crafts, playing musical instruments, writing poems, reciting poems, creating comedies, photography, handling technical issues, cooking, organizing others, preaching, and a whole lot more. Just like coaches scouting for potential college athletes attend different high school track meets and watch the students engage in their sports, so do we need to observe and listen to children in their natural environments and pick out their talents.

For some children, their talents manifest early in our encounter with them, while others come up later. Jordan was in my midweek service class in CEIC in Chesapeake, Virginia, and for two years, I did not pick up her talent. During the third and last year of our stay in the church, she blossomed into this powerful soprano singer that I wished could come along with us to York when we were leaving so that I would continue to train her. On the other hand, the first day I got to RCCG York children's Sunday school, I identified Sarah, Bella, and Savannah as gifted children in different areas, and by the second Sunday, I started working with Sarah and Bella to present a poem that I wrote for the Mothers' Day. Since then, we have discovered more talents in the class.

Singing and voice training

Osaretin was one of the children in my class in RCCG House of Praise in Chesapeake, Virginia, who asked insightful questions. He was very friendly and playful. One day, this chubby nine-year-old was playing and making fun of some singers when I discovered beyond the din of the noise and laughter that he had a beautiful and rich operatic voice. Eureka!

I had never heard a child that young sing in such mature baritone. We went to work right away. We gave him voice training, and as he grew older, the gem in his voice came alive. It has been more than six years since we left the church, but Osaretin's soulful rendition of *Amazing Grace* will wake me up from the deepest sleep any day. I just love his golden voice. There are children who may have the talent but are not ready for exposure to the public. We work with them quietly to ensure that their talents are developed but keep them in the background until they are ready. One of such children was Funsho. She had a sonorous soprano voice covering a huge range, and as young as she was when I discovered her talent, I wanted her to be one of the lead singers in our group. She was too shy and not ready. I waited for her for six years before giving her that role. Along the way, I paired her up with other children until I was certain that she could handle the lead role. Isabel was another child that had what I considered an award-winning voice, but she would not go on stage to sing. I spoke with her, cajoled, quoted scriptures, encouraged, advised, and did whatever I could to help her gain some confidence, all to no avail. She simply would not sing before an audience. I let her be.

There are others whose talents do not shine to catch your

attention because they are eclipsed by other stars in the same training program. If they are in the right environment, they will shine when their time is ripe. Bukky was such a star. For all the time she was in our Happiness Club program, she was never a lead singer. She sang in the group, more like a back-up. After graduating from Happiness Club, Bukky (Google Bouqui) obtained her bachelor's degree and got a job in a radio station as a producer. Years later, she felt a calling to be a full-time professional gospel artist. She quit her job and has been performing as a gospel artist. She has won many national and international music awards. She has also pro-duced several albums and writes her own songs.

(a) Musical Instruments

It is not only in singing that we have discovered and de-veloped the talents of the children. With the exception of CEIC, we have run annual summer music workshops in the churches that we have been privileged to serve since we emigrated to the United States. We hire professional and non-professional instrumentalists to teach our children for a period of two to three weeks on different musical instru-ments. Thereafter, we follow up with their parents to ensure that the children continue to practice the instruments of their choice. In some cases, the children continue by getting tu-torials from YouTube. Our twins Mika (Chiemika) and DD

(Chiedozie) participated in some of the summer music work-shops in Maryland, where they learned to play the guitar. When we got to Chesapeake, they got tutorials from You-Tube and honed their skills. Both are so skilled in playing rhythm and bass guitars, respectively. They can play for pro-fessional bands. We have also engaged them as resource peo-ple during our workshops. Jack, Kachi, Nosa, Jayden, Ewa, Sarah, Enayemen, Abigail-1, Asher, Michael, Amarachi, Abigail-2, Tayo, Soma, Itoro, and many others developed their talents during these summer music workshops. Some of them now play for their respective church and fellowship choirs or bands. One approach we have adopted is to engage our students in training the next set of instrumentalists in our peer mentoring program. The success of this program is that a pipeline of instrumentalists is created, which ensures that the church does not lack instrumentalists. For our TEEM-ED purpose, developing these musical talents and channeling them to serve the Lord in churches and fellowships ensure that the children are engaged and serving the Lord in an en-vironment where they continually grow by hearing the Word of God.

(b) Choreography and dance

I do not know how to teach anybody to dance because I am not endowed in that area. However, we have other members of our team who are exceptionally talented in choreography and dance. They work with the children to develop these talents. In CEIC, my colleague Erika Swindell raised one of the best choreography groups that I have ever watched perform. Her daughter Jaeda is a phenomenal dancer who has won several awards in regional competitions. She is a major contributor to the great successes of the choreography team in CEIC. Jaeda is also incredibly talented. Not only does she dance, but she also creates the dance moves and teaches her peers. Once on the dance stage during rehearsals, the twelve-year-old, home-schooled prodigy would turn into a generalissimo, marshaling her troops, instructing, directing, and coaching her peers. The group definitely is of national and international quality. When we arrived in York, Pennsylvania, we gave the responsibility to raise a standard choreography group to two high school teenagers (Joyce and Halima) in our Youth Church. They did. Soon, one of the twelve-year-olds, Savannah, became our Jaeda in York. Just like Jaeda, Savannah would create, teach, and direct the other kids on the choreography, initially under the supervision of Joyce and Halima. When Joyce went to college, she worked virtually with Savannah to create the dance moves which Savannah taught the other kids. The team of Joyce and Halima, with Savannah as their arrowhead, has created a choreography group in steps with the CEIC group.

(c) Drama: Acting and writing

I have a passion for communicating the Word of God using drama as the medium or vehicle for sharing the gospel message and promoting quality Christian living. I was involved in our Scripture Union drama group right after my high school, but it was at the University of Ife that my acting and writing skills were honed. I did not study theater arts, but we were blessed to have fellow students in our ECU drama group who brought a professional flair to the quality of plays that we acted. Besides, during my undergraduate and grad school days at Ife, the university had one of the best performing arts troupes in the country under the direction of the Nobel Laureate, Professor Wole Soyinka. We watched their performances, and I learned a lot from them. I joined the ECU drama group right from the first week of my freshman year and acted in several plays, including *Too Hard to Handle* and *No Resting Place There*. The plays were written by the students and were of such a high standard that I was told that Wole Soyinka would clear his schedule to watch plays by the ECU drama group.

The training I got in this group in four years prepared me for a lifetime of writing, producing, and directing drama pieces and concerts both for children and adults. In recent times, we have been writing and producing Christmas concerts in the churches that we have been privileged to serve. This has afforded us the uncommon opportunity of discovering and developing the talents of the children that are gifted in drama. Not only do we give them scripted plays to perform, we often ask them to create the drama pieces by themselves. As I stated in an earlier chapter, part of our regular Sunday school schedule incorporates a time for the children to work in groups and come up with skits which they work on and present to the class. These regular drama presentations help us to identify the children who are gifted in either creating or acting plays. We mentor them and help them shine in this area.

(d) Crafts and cooking

Much as we encourage men to be in charge of their families, we are well aware that women contribute significantly to the stability of the home. Sometime in 2014, the Lord laid it on my wife's heart to create a program specifically for the girls in our children's Sunday school. She started a program called the Dorcas Club. Her focus was to raise girls of exceptional integrity who would be the center of gravity of their future homes. She took the children through different kinds of crafts: she taught them knitting, crocheting, and basic sewing. She also taught them how to cook and serve several simple dishes as well as basic table etiquettes. Occasionally, other ladies joined her to teach the children different dishes and crafts. The sessions were held in our home. Parents dropped off their children at specified times and came back for them later. The session started off with a Bible study, after which they would do the craft for the day. It was a hands-on exercise. Each child had her own tool kit and followed instructions. After the crafts session, the children proceeded to prepare a meal which they shared together. The children participated in preparing the ingredients. Occasionally, the older ones did the cooking under strict supervision. Different recipes were taught. The girls enjoyed the experience. The mealtime seemed to be the best part of the day. The girls were taught how to set a table for formal dinner to the minute details of where to place the cutlery and napkins. They were taught how to sit down properly at the table, which hand to hold the table knife and the fork (or spoon depending on the dish), how to pray before meals, and how to enjoy the meal without hurrying off in two minutes. Cleaning up after the meal was carefully supervised, and every child participated in it. It was a grooming session. Most of the children came into the program not knowing how to do much, but within three months, the transformation was evident. A strong bond was developed between the teacher and the pupils. Parents were grateful for this extra training their children received. Some parents who were not members of our church brought their daughters to participate in the program. During special occasions like Mother's Day or Father's Day, the children were taught to create unique gifts for their parents. They were taught that special gifts did not have to cost a lot of money. This special mentoring for girls is highly recommended in our TEEM-ED model of children's ministry. We care for the overall development of the child. We are also interested in little things that make for stability in the home, which ultimately will affect their faith in the future.

(e) Field trips and educational tours

When I ask graduates of our Sunday school what aspects of our programs impacted their lives the most, field trips or tours rank among the topmost three. We did not design field trips as part of our curriculum originally. It was an outgrowth of the talent discovery and development program that we pursued in Happiness Club in the early eighties. We developed a unique children's choir in Happiness Club. Initially, the choir sang in the chapel occasionally, but with time, it was exposed to a national platform that gave our group huge publicity. We got invitations to minister in different churches and programs outside the city of Ife. Traveling became part of our experience. We discovered that beyond the ministrations, traveling together in a bus was fun for the kids and experiences that they later told me they cherished the most. They bonded well and developed relationships that helped their walk with the Lord. It was also a time for the teachers to get to know the children outside the four walls of the classroom. The beneficial experience was mutual. Based on this realization, we made field trips one of the major pillars of our TEEM-ED program.

One of the places we visited in the United States is the Holy Land Experience in Florida. We took the children from Chesapeake in Virginia to Florida. I believe that it was an experience that they would like to relive any day. We drove all the way from Chesapeake to Florida. The journey took us about thirteen hours because we had a couple of bathroom breaks and lunchtime. One mistake we made was to allow three six-year-old children to travel with us. They created some anxiety moments for us. When we arrived at the hotel where we slept for the night, the children were excited that we had finally arrived in Florida after the long journey. They all rushed out of the vehicle to the lobby while we were checking in. We did a headcount and discovered that one of the children was missing. It was scary. We later found her in one of the vans, comfortably asleep. Another one followed some of the bigger children and took the staircase instead of the elevator. Somewhere up the stairwell, they outran and left her on her own. Confused and not knowing what to do, she simply sat down on one of the floors and created scary moments for us.

The trip was expensive for our small church to sponsor. We did a little fund-raiser, and our pastor was able to connect with a pastor friend of his in Florida who made it a memorable experience for the children and all the teachers. Despite the logistical challenges we had during this trip, the Holy Land Experience trip was one the children will not be in a hurry to forget. It is a place to visit.

In 2019, we took the children in our church in York, Pennsylvania, to the Museum of the Bible in Washington D.C. This time, we made sure that we did not take any child younger than eight years of age. It was both an educational trip and a fun experience for the children. They checked out thousands of artifacts in the museum, attended talks, and had movie sessions. For the younger children (four to seven years old), we took them to Banyard Farms in Lancaster, about twenty minutes away from our church. They, too, had fun and a huge lunch to boot. We planned a visit to Billy Graham's library in Charlotte, North Carolina, and Sight and Sound Theater in Lancaster but could not go because of the pandemic. By God's grace, we shall still take the children to these places. We are considering some Christian businesses and higher institutions to take the children to. The idea is to take them to institutions, theaters, businesses, and museums with strong Christian history and ethics. We may never know what impact any visit will have on their walk with the Lord and their overall development. All we can do is sow the seed and allow the Lord to give the increase.

(f) Outreaches and ministrations

Preparing the children for service in the Lord's vineyard is a major focus of the TEEM-ED model of children's ministry. As we develop the children's talents, the goal is to channel them to the service of the Lord. Our approach is to create opportunities for ministry for the children starting from their home church. Children's Day, Mother's Day, Father's Day, Easter, Christmas concert, and other occasions provide perfect avenues to train them in ministry. We emphasize to them that they are primarily ministers and not entertainers. With time, that message sinks in, and the children recognize that anytime they go on stage to present a song, recite a poem or memory verses, present a skit, or even preach, it is not about them. It is about sharing the gospel message with the audience. They are doing the Lord's work and should expect rewards from the Lord. That does not mean that the audience should not clap for them. We encourage the audience to appreciate them; after all, they are still children and cherish any encouragement that they could get from people. However, they are trained to acknowledge that their gifts and talents are from the Lord, and it is a noble thing to turn those endowments into the service of the Lord.

Beyond ministering in their local church, we seek opportunities for the children to minister in other churches, fellowships, and Christian concerts. We encourage children's ministries to create programs and invite other children's churches and ministries to participate. From our experience, it is advisable to avoid creating competitions if other churches are involved, and prizes will be awarded. Occasionally, in the quest to have the children from their church win (at all cost), some teachers succumb to the temptation of cheating. The children will see through it and have bad memories of such competitions. I remember an invitation that we accepted to participate in a church program. As it turned out, there was a panel of judges that evaluated the performance of the children that had been invited from different churches. By the time the children from our church presented, the audience knew that they were way beyond the other groups' performances. Unfortunately, the judges who were predominantly from the host church did less than justice to their assessment of the performances. They awarded the first position to the children from the host church and the second position to our children. When the results were announced, people were shocked. Even children from the host church protested the decision. Our children were wounded because they saw a display of flagrant injustice on that day. After that experience, we resolved not to accept any invitation to a competition organized by a church except the judges are neutral individuals, preferably not affiliated to any of the competing churches. We would rather accept invitations to simply minister. Our focus is to prepare the children to transition seamlessly to any callings that the Lord may have on their lives in the future.

Just like the field trips, the ministrations and outreaches are equally occasions when the children travel together in groups. They love it. The difference here is that, unlike the field trips during which they are the recipients of information and knowledge, they are on the giving end during outreaches. They prepare well and make sacrifices to be able to be in the state in which God can use them effectively. They go through grilling and intense rehearsals and often spend time in prayer and fasting before any major outreach. We encourage them to fast but do not insist on it. However, most of the children do fast from morning till noon as they prepare to minister both locally in the church or other places that they are invited to. Often, the presence of God during their ministrations is unmistakable. I remember one ministration that was so powerful. God used it to birth a ministry that has transformed the lives of hundreds, if not thousands of individuals to this day. This happened in the 3000-seat auditorium in the University of Ife (Nigeria) called Oduduwa Hall in the eighties. We had our church service in this auditorium, and the Happiness Club sang one of our original compositions—*Heaven My Precious City.* The lead singer, ten-year-old Oluchi, took a solo which goes like this:

In Heaven, there'll be love and peace and joy

No crying, no sickness, no struggling, no pain

There will be light from the Lord, ever shining
It's my home; I'll be there someday

Something extraordinary happened. Oluchi's face glowed with heavenly beauty as she looked up as if she were in a trance and having direct communication with the Lord. The girl was in a different realm of glory. Her angelic voice sliced through the quiet reverence that pervaded the auditorium that morning as she belted out the soul-piercing song in her rich soprano. I was not prepared for what followed; neither was the audience. The ten-year-old burst out crying as she was rounding off the solo. Another girl tried to help but also joined in the crying. Before we knew it, most of the singers were crying. The tears flowed, and I suspect that there were not a few tears in the audience. I was conducting the song and managed to take it to the end. When we left the stage, the tears continued to flow.

As I was writing this story, I felt like finding out from Oluchi if she remembered this experience. I wanted to know why she cried that morning. She certainly did, as if it were yesterday. Now a chartered accountant, entrepreneur, and a mother of eleven, nineteen, and twenty-year-old boys, Oluchi picked up my call on the first dial and, with nostalgic excitement, recounted to me what happened to her that morning. She said to me, "Of course, I do. When I sang 'Heaven' that day, I felt like a cloud (of glory) settled on the audience, and people were being slain in the spirit. Each time I sing 'Heaven,' I feel like I am in a different realm, and I cannot stop the tears. It happens to me up till today."

The Holy Spirit was in the room to anoint someone for service. The anointing was heavy. Unknown to us, one of the doctors in our medical center was sitting in the audience that morning. After our ministration, he could not stay in the auditorium anymore. He left the church service and went to the sports center about three blocks away. I was told that he lay flat on the ground crying unto the Lord, asking Him what He would have him do. If God could touch children that young the way He did that morning, He could use the doctor for His glory. Dr. Orioke came out from that encounter, a changed man. God anointed him and used him as the founder of one of the largest evangelical ministries in the city of Ife.

Something similar happened many years later when we took the children from Bethel Fellowship Church in Glendale, Maryland, to minister in New Covenant Church in Hyattsville, Maryland. The children sang with passion and recited the poem *Beyond His Passion* with such zeal and conviction, and the Holy Spirit took over. Some members of the church, including a professor of Chemistry at Howard University, cried as we ministered that morning.

The TEEM-ED model of children's ministry is a comprehensive approach to ministering to children with a singular outcome in view—to train up a child to become and continue as a committed Christian all the days of his life. We lay emphasis on:

1. Leading a child to Christ.

2. Getting a child baptized in the Holy Spirit.

3. Discipling a child.

4. Discovering and developing the talent(s) of a child.

5. Channeling a child's talent to the service of the Lord.

6. Preparing a child to transition into an effective witness for the Lord.

7. Creating an enabling environment for a child to grow to his full potentials.

8. Providing responsible mentoring that helps a child navigate through life with confidence.

9. Providing a fun environment where children learn to love and respect one another and,

10. Providing activities that promote lasting friendships among our children.

It is contemporary in approach and drills an all-around target of excellence into the consciousness of a child. It is intentional. We do not do children's ministry as a hobby. We take the call seriously. We train our teachers to model Christianity to the children. We organize seminars to equip the teachers with up-to-date information on children's ministry. Our motto is "Sunday school is fun," and our tagline is "We are kids, but we are not kidding." Through field trips, drama, singing, playing musical instruments, photography, poetry recitals, etc., we engage the interests of the children, providing a fertile and friendly environment that promotes the scriptural principles that we teach them to grow and flourish.

In writing this book, I considered it necessary to include reflections of a few of the "children" who have passed through our program on the impact that it had on their lives. To have a cross-sectional view, representing different cohorts of the children that were in our program, we reached out to different blocks. I have included here some of the responses I got from "children" that we taught ten, twenty, thirty, and forty years ago, as well as those we are teaching currently. Come along with me and let us see what they have.

A Life-transforming Encounter: Dr. Paul Aliu (Senior executive at Novartis HQ in Switzerland)

I spent a chunk of my childhood in the idyllic University campus in Ife—a beautifully landscaped twenty-square kilometer space designed by the famous Israeli architect Ariel Sharon. Among other things, the campus had its own museums, zoo, dam, botanical gardens, theaters, sports center, multiple architectural masterpieces, and a collection of some of the most intelligent minds across various fields.

In the early eighties, shortly after my family moved back to Nigeria from Manchester, I was one of about ten kids brought together on a Saturday to sing and make music under the tutelage of a talented and enthusiastic Sunday School teacher—Uncle 'Inno' as we fondly called him, who was a pharmacy post-graduate student at the University of Ife. It was probably an activity our parents shipped us to primarily to keep us busy on a Saturday afternoon, and let's face it, a bit of music with religion cannot be so bad for hyperactive growing young children. However, little did they know (neither did we) that this single course of action will define and shape our destinies.

"Happiness Club," as the group was known, played a pivotal role at a very impressionable phase of my life. Every Saturday, I gathered with friends, who would all later become like family, sang my heart out, learned the rudiments of vocal singing (e.g., breathing, harmonies, voice projection, and performance), acting, playing musical instruments, and more importantly, had the word of God etched in my heart through the power of music. The club will later grow to have hundreds of kids, who will dutifully turn up every week for practice and regularly perform in churches and music festivals across the country. Who can forget our tagline—"We are kids, but we are not kidding!"

Two experiences that have stayed with me over the years were the visitation of the Holy Spirit in the Sunday School class (at the All Souls Chapel) and at a Happiness Club session (in preparation for the Living Spring music festival), both with Uncle Inno. The presence of the Holy Spirit was so tangible in the room on both occasions, with some of those present breaking into tongues, healing, praying, and worshipping totally unbridled—something special was happening right there. It was our own "upper room" experience as a bunch of children; all felt unleashed and empowered to take on the world and spread the message fearlessly.

In the autumn of 1985, I headed off to a boarding school in Abuja, the newly designated capital city of Nigeria at the time, over 500 kilometers away from home and Happiness Club. In Abuja, among many other new activities I took up, I very quickly signed up for the school choir, joined the school fellowship choir, and was teaching a whole bunch of keen young singers from all parts of Nigeria the many Happiness Club songs I had spent my Saturday afternoons belting out! I would, over the years, become the school choirmaster/conductor and a member of the school band, playing the lead guitar.

Fast forward some forty years afterward; I am a board-certified pharmacist with a clinical doctorate, a law degree, and an executive MBA, an award-winning poet, working as a senior executive at the headquarters of one of the world's largest pharmaceutical companies. I have been blessed to be at the cutting edge of medicine, with the opportunity to lead various global therapeutic development programs for diseases including cancer, organ transplantation, rheumatoid arthritis, malaria, and rare genetic diseases. I am passionate about global health, health equity, and access to medicines. I regularly write and speak on these topics at various international think-tanks and conferences. I now live about 5,000 kilometers from Ife, in another idyllic part of the world, having studied, lived, and worked in many countries and pretty much all continents (with the exception of Antarctica!).

I very often reflect on the impact Sunday school and Happiness Club have had on my life—the gift of music and poetry, the grounding of my faith, the art of performance, stage confidence, a heart of service, and the ability to share the gospel and my ministry irrespective of age, race, creed, and geography. The songs we sang back then have ministered to me at different times over the years and continue to do. I am currently a worship leader at my local church, a non-denominational international church in Switzerland, with members from over seventy countries.

Many thanks to Uncle Inno and his dear wife, our very own Aunty Vicky, for heeding the call of God on their lives to teach, nurture and impact children from diverse homes in Ife, Port Harcourt, and more recently in the United States, ultimately impacting many more homes, churches, and societies across the globe. It is not surprising how many of us "Happiness Club kids" are now leading professionals in various fields and worship leaders, Sunday School teachers, and pastors in our local churches. A Happiness Club song that comes to mind is:

> Let's work together for God
> Walking together in harmony
> Together we will overcome the world
> With the tools of our profession and the Word

Thanks to Happiness Club for the seed sown and nurtured from that early age. While I am still a work in progress, I feel equipped to overcome the world with the "tools" of my profession and the Word!

Dr. Paul Aliu is the Head of Global Governance in the cross-divisional Chief Medical Office (CMO) at the headquarters of Novartis in Switzerland.

Changed for Eternity: *Kemi Ogunsan (A medical doctor and Sunday school teacher)*

Keep step with the Master, whatever betide;

Though dark be the pathway, keep close to your Guide,

While foes are alluring, and danger is near,

When walking with Jesus, you've nothing to fear.

Refrain:

Keeping step go bravely forward,

And thy courage will renew;

Daily walk with Christ your Saviour,

He will lead you all the journey through.

Keep step with the Master, wherever you go;

Through darkness and shadow the way He will show,

The light of His presence your path will illume,

And make all the desert a garden of bloom. [Refrain]

Keep step with the Master, nor halt by the way;

Whate'er He commands you, oh, haste to obey!

Arise at His bidding, press on in His might;

While walking with Jesus, you're sure to be right. [Refrain]"

Written by Fanny Crosby

I was eleven years old when Uncle Innocent taught us this hymn in Sunday school. It never left me.

I still sing it today—knocking at the door of fifty, and over the years, the Lord has brought it to mind to encourage me to keep walking with Jesus through thick and thin.

It's amazing the role music has played in my spiritual upbringing and journey, from hearing my mom sing, "Steal away to Jesus," "Let all the world in every corner sing my God and King," and other hymns from six to seven years of age, to learning Happiness Club songs in 1980-81, and singing choruses, hymns and spirituals at the beginning of Sunday school class Sunday after Sunday.

It's so vivid in my memory like it was yesterday, the day Uncle Innocent taught us, "O brother have you told how the Lord forgave, let us hear you tell it over once again" (by John M Whyte) along with its tonic solfa, *s: d: d: d: d: m:s:s: l: d: s:- s: s: d: d: d: d: d: d: t: d: r:-:-* etc.

Three of my dear friends and I habitually sat in front of Sunday school class those days and sang with enthusiasm and joy. We were also taught and encouraged to memorize Bible verses every Sunday school class. Who can forget "Tall Uncle George Alao" (another wonderful Sunday school teacher) and the Sunday school anniversary when Ebun (nee Togun) flawlessly recited Jesus sermon on the mount (Matthew chapters five, six, and seven) at a very tender age. Uncle George was standing there on the sidelines, spurring her on till she uttered the last word, and the auditorium erupted in applause.

For a few years, I fluctuated in my commitment to the Lord, then after rededicating my life to Christ in 1986, I joined the church choir and learned songs like,

If God is dead

What makes the flowers bloom

If God is dead

What makes summer come in June

If God Is dead

Who is listening and who answers prayers

I'm so glad I know

God Lives, He Lives, He lives

He Lives, He Lives

If God is dead

Who can mends a broken heart

If God is dead

What makes night and day apart

If God is dead

Who can tell me where His body lies

I'm glad I know

God Lives, he Lives, He lives

God Lives In me

I can feel him moving

Through the trees and the wind

And the breeze

I can see him shinning

Thru the night and the stars

that shine so bright

If God is Dead

What makes my life worth living

I'm glad I know He lives

He lives (X5)

By Mighty Clouds of Joy

Within months Uncle Innocent invited me to come back to Sunday school, but this time as a teacher. He gave me the scripture for my first lesson, 1 Corinthians 15:58, "Therefore my beloved brethren, be ye steadfast, unmovable, always abounding in the work of the Lord, for as much as ye know that your labor is not in vain in the Lord."

The verse stuck with me, and I've remained a Sunday school teacher ever since.

Along the way, I discovered Maranatha Music and had the privilege of attending Living Spring yearly (an annual national Christian music festival held in Ile-Ife, Nigeria) from 1983 to date. I remember traveling to Lagos as an "aunty" with Happiness Club, once when they went to minister at a concert, alongside Pacelli school for the blind choir. The presence of God was so tangible you could cut it with a knife.

Why start my contribution to Uncle's book with the above? I thought, rather than simply write a laundry list of "Effective teaching strategies for Sunday school, teachers," perhaps I could bear witness to what my Sunday school teachers did that influenced me (and others) for a lifetime, no, for eternity. Indeed, the power of influence one Sunday school teacher can have is profound. Only eternity will tell the impact Uncle Innocent and Uncle George had on me and many others I grew up with—simply because they decided to teach Sunday school. They did not relegate the task to women. They did not despise it or despise us. They taught us in all earnestness, as unto the Lord.

As I cast my mind back, I realize that it was more than just the songs and the teaching; it was their love for the Lord and consequently for us that translated into this deep, lasting life-transforming influence on us. They prayed for us, visited some while they were in boarding school, invited us to their homes after they got married; their wives became our "aunties" and joined them in ministering to us. They encouraged us to use our gifts to serve the Lord. The musically inclined among us were encouraged to write their own songs. They prayed for us and for our families. They stayed in touch and inquired about our Christian walk, our education through university, and our careers beyond. Did I mention that they prayed for us? Yes, they never stopped praying for us. The Holy Spirit worked through them to draw us to Christ and grow us in Him.

At that time, we didn't have computers, mobile phones, social media, and all the attractions and distractions that come with today's technology. But I dare say, the "basic tools" they used to reach us remain the best and most effective for Sunday school teachers in any era—*love, care, time, prayer, the Word of God, sharing of themselves, inviting us into their homes—the Holy Spirit* moved them to touch and stay in our lives, and they did.

The practical tools the Lord leads Sunday school teachers to use may differ from generation to generation. For mine, music was integral to and effective in leading us to Christ and teaching us His word. For other "generations," techno-giz, social media, strobe lights, etc., may be employed.

Whatever the practical tools—without the *Holy Spirit*, without the *undiluted Word of God*, without the sacrifice of *love, time, prayer, and care*, without the authenticity of lives lived for and before the Lord transparently—the practical tools will be to no avail. The fruit will not abide.

May the Lord raise a new generation of Sunday school teachers (especially men) who, "Keep step with the Master whatever betide," and lead others to do likewise.

Thank you, Uncle Innocent, Uncle George, Aunty Vickie, Aunty Omolade. Thank you for giving to the Lord. Our lives were changed.

Dr. Kemi Ogunsan (MD) is the Director of Children's Ministry in New Covenant Church Hyattsville, Maryland.

A life positively impacted and influenced: Yemi Adeyemo (Accountant and pastor)

My name is Yemi Adeyemo. I serve as an associate pastor in Kingdom Ambassadors Christian Center (KACC) in Maryland. I am the minister in charge of the choir and the prayer group in this assembly. I desire that as many people as possible will come to the saving knowledge of Christ. I use any opportunity I have to encourage believers to embrace the finished works of Christ in its entirety.

One of the people that influenced me most in a positive way as I was growing up was Dr. Innocent Ononiwu. We fondly call him Uncle Innocent. I was privileged to be taught and impacted by this wonderful and God-fearing man at the Sunday school (children's church) of All Souls Chapel in the University of Ife (now OAU) in Nigeria.

Let me share some ways I was positively influenced by Uncle Innocent: As a child that was keenly observing my teachers, I noticed that he exemplified the things that he taught us. So, it was easy to emulate him without the fear of being misled. He had a flair and an ear for music: that was one tool he deployed effectively to teach and impact the lives of the children.

We thought that Uncle Innocent started Happiness Club; I never knew the person who started it. The only person we knew that groomed us in this activity group was Uncle Innocent: Happiness Club is a group for children that he met with regularly with the purpose of introducing them to biblical teachings. This club helped identify and develop musical talents that were later deployed to minister Christ through songs and melodious music. I was in Happiness club at some point.

Uncle started another outreach program called BUBBLE (acronym for Burdens Unloaded Bountiful Blessings let Loose Extraordinarily). The purpose of this program was to reach teenagers, to bring them to the saving knowledge of Christ. Also, it helped to strengthen and encourage believers not to waiver but stay strong in their faith in Christ Jesus. I was heavily involved in this program.

Over the years, Uncle Innocent has been consistent and steadfast in his ministry to children. Wherever he goes, he leaves his trademark, which is teaching and impacting children with the knowledge of Christ. This he does by teaching them God's Word and helping discover their talents. Thanks for yielding yourself to God. I am a life that has been impacted and positively influenced.

Pastor Yemi is an accountant. He is also an associate pastor with Kingdom Ambassadors Christian Center in Landover, Maryland.

Impact of Happiness Club on me: Dr. Nnenna Ugorji *(Pediatrician)*

As a young child, growing up in a university environment, I had the opportunity of interacting with so many other kids at school and at several other activities on campus. We also met in church during what we called Sunday school. These activities were always fun, and we really looked forward to them.

One of such groups which I was blessed to be a part of was a group called Happiness Club, developed by a graduate student in the Faculty of Pharmacy of the University of Ife, Innocent Ononiwu, whom we popularly referred to as "Uncle Inno," a name we still address him by today.

Uncle Inno, together with some other Christian uncles and aunties, would gather us every Saturday at 4 p.m. Most of us who gathered were children of faculty and staff of the university. This meeting was the highlight of most of our weeks.

We learned and sang gospel songs composed by Uncle Inno. He grouped us in parts (treble, alto, tenor, etc.) to sing in harmony. We also had Bible studies, participated in arts and crafts, and had fellowship with one another in such heartwarming ways. Our singing did not end there as we went ahead to sing in churches on invitation as well as in the annual Living Spring Festival held in Ile-Ife, which was attended by gospel artists from around the world.

285

I remember with delight our brown and white uniforms and how smart we all looked as we got in "formation" in readiness for our presentations. Our choir was frequently made up of a wide range of children from preschoolers, grade school kids, the preteens to teenagers. Everyone was welcome, and we all had a place. We also had instrumentalists who were students of the University of Ife, whom Uncle Inno brought along to play for us when we had engagements. It was an all-around experience, one that we missed so much when my family later moved to one of the eastern states in Nigeria.

As I reflect, over three decades later, on the impact that Happiness Club had on my life, one of the things that stands out is the hunger it created in me from a very young age for the things of God. The environment Uncle Inno and his wife, Aunty Vickie, created was one of joy in being in God's presence, enjoying the warmth and fellowship of others, discovering our gifts, learning that we could serve God with our talents, and cultivating our individual faiths. I don't recall ever being coerced to accept Jesus Christ as Lord and Savior in any of our meetings but what I do remember is that as we met and learned about Him, sang our hearts out to Him, and fellowshipped with each other, my heart became receptive, and I would eventually discover my own faith and begin my personal walk with Jesus with little or no persuasion from anyone but from being exposed early in my home and by the influence of Happiness Club.

In all my life's experiences, no matter what I have faced, the one thing I have carried along with me has been my faith. Knowing Jesus from a very young age has been my life's greatest treasure and has anchored me through the changing scenes of life, in my family, my relationships, and in my career.

Can I also mention the exposure I gained in worshipping God in songs, which has helped me serve Him and the church with my gifts in the different countries we've called home (Trinidad and Tobago, Jersey, Nigeria, Channels Islands, and the United Kingdom)? None of this would have been possible without the strong influence of Happiness Club. The songs we learned back then are still so relevant today, teaching timeless lessons, some of which I've gone on to teach my own children.

I am hugely indebted to Uncle Inno for the deposits he made in my life through his service in Happiness Club. The harvest from it is one he would reap for a lifetime and when we all see Jesus face to face.

Dr Nnenna Ugoji is a pediatrician. She works at the North Cumbria Integrated Care NHS Foundation Trust, United Kingdom.

Great Sunday school: *Lenu Apapa (Senior magistrate)*

My name is Lenu Apapa. I am a senior magistrate with the Rivers State Judiciary in Port-Harcourt, Rivers State, Nigeria. I am married with two lovely kids. My church for as long as I can remember and even till now has been Our Saviour's Chapel, the University of Port-Harcourt (in Nigeria). One outstanding department of this church is our vibrant children's Sunday school. Sunday school was where we were taught the principles that have guided my life up till today. The Sunday school had two activity groups, Happiness Club and later Young Talents Club for teenagers (both were started by Uncle Innocent in the University of Port-Harcourt). Uncle Innocent Ononiwu was one of the teachers who affected my life in Sunday School. His teaching got to me because it was never an abstract message. He always taught with real-life examples either from his own experiences or from those around him. So, it was easy to put those scriptural lessons into practical daily life experiences. I still remember when he told us not to give the devil a landing pad in our lives. I learned practical Christianity in our children's Sunday school, and it still guides me today. "Keep me shining Lord" was one of the songs that kept me going.

Uncle Innocent also taught us some great songs (most of which he and his wife, Auntie Vickie, composed) which are being sung by my own children years after. To complete the circle, I am now the head of that same Sunday school where Uncle Innocent taught me over twenty years ago. I pray that the children under me will have as much fun learning about God as I did through Uncle Innocent's teaching.

His Lordship Lenu Apapa is a senior magistrate (the equivalent of a district court judge in the United States) in the Rivers State judiciary in Nigeria.

The things we learned did not leave us: *Chidiuto Cobb JD (Recent law school graduate)*

As a student in my dad's Sunday school classes over the years, the thing that probably impacted me the most was "insights." When we had a scripture or lesson in Sunday school, he would always ask us for our insights. This was an opportunity for us to bring all our different experiences to the table and really ask the question, "What does this mean in *my* life?" This did a few things. First, it made the Bible applicable in a way that we could all understand. When the lesson was summarized in my own voice or in the voices of my peers, it went much further than just a teacher talking *at* you. Second, it helped me understand that what I said and thought was important and relevant. Even when we didn't understand something, we were allowed to express ourselves and then got redirected to what was correct. I learned from making mistakes sometimes and sometimes getting it right.

Third, because we had to write out our insights, the things we learned did not just leave us when we left the church building. The lessons lasted even longer than when we had those notebooks to look back on. Lastly, by having to ask what the passage meant in our lives, it meant that the Bible truly has something to say about my life. This gave us many opportunities to respond to what the Bible said and see the benefits of following Jesus at an early age. Today, I am still using these skills and lessons, yes, in my relationship with God, but also in my education and career. Now finishing my last year of law school, I have seen how the confidence I gained from reading the scripture, thinking about its application, and writing out the lessons I learned, has positively impacted me throughout my life.

Chidiuto Cobb (one of the author's daughters) is a graduate of the Howard University School of Law. After graduating from Duke University, she spent one year doing missionary work with Every Nation.

Life-Changing Concepts: *Kelechi Eluchie (Medical laboratory scientist)*

Growing up in the early 2000s, Sunday mornings were eventful. Rushing to get ready for church, my parents ensured that my siblings and I were clean and dressed in our

"Sunday best," that our hair was neatly brushed and in place, and that our Bibles and journals were packed and ready to go. I'm sure other parents also fussed over their children because they looked well-groomed. As my family and other families arrived at church, our parents would drop us in the children's Sunday school and then proceed to join the adult service. Children were assigned to one of three classes based on age—Genesis, Proverbs, or Revelations. Revelations Class, also known as the Next Generation Revelation (NGR) at the time, was the childhood Sunday school class that made the most impact in my life. Little did all our parents know that all the young ribbon and bow tie-clad children they left in "children's church" were being well-equipped for a lifetime of ministry and service to God.

Although Uncle Innocent and his team were teaching nine-to twelve-year-olds in NGR, they did not treat us like children. Studying the Bible and recording what Uncle Innocent called "insights" were a regular part of the class. He would assign us a scripture to read and meditate on, and after some minutes, would ask us to share with the rest of the class what we understood from the scripture. While this might seem like a simple exercise, it challenged me to study the Word of God for understanding and application and not just read superficially. The Bible says to "Train up a child in the way he should go, and when he is old, he will not depart from it" (Proverbs 22:6, NKJV). I believe that this

291

is what Uncle Innocent did with us in his class, and I still see its impact on my life as an adult today. It was during those sessions that my gifts of writing and understanding and explaining the Word of God were discovered—Uncle Innocent would often highlight those gifts. Years later, I began to write scripture-based blogs and have been serving as a Bible study teacher in various settings. Our Sunday school "insight" sessions have continued to bear much fruit. Uncle Innocent's class is a gift that keeps on giving.

Weekly homework assignments were a part of this gift that keeps on giving. My NGR classmates and I were assigned different weekly memory verses, which we were to practice during the week. The following Sunday, we were asked to recite our assigned scriptures from memory. The importance of knowing and remembering God's Word was highly emphasized in our class. I still recall the lesson about the armor of God (Ephesians 6:10-18); the vivid explanations and cartoon-like illustrations in class helped it to stick in my memory. The concept of being equipped to stand firm in the evil day taught me that there would be times when one may not have a physical Bible available; therefore, it would be the memorized and understood Word of God that would carry one through the challenge. There are several other concepts and scriptures that Uncle Innocent encouraged us to commit to memory. Another one that comes to mind is "Others may, but I cannot." That short but loaded phrase has remained with me and helped instill in me the importance of practicing integrity as a Christian. I have kept my notes from over a decade ago and revisit them occasionally. As I review those notes, I am in awe of the lessons I was blessed to learn at such a young age.

While scripture reading, memorization, and application were taught, creativity was a key component of our Sunday school classes. Uncle Innocent's classes were filled with group projects, where we created original skits, poems, raps, and songs. He took it a step further and arranged for us to minister these productions at our church, during conferences, and at other churches. We even recorded a musical CD. Sometimes, prizes were attached to our performance, which motivated us to get more creative in our presentations. Because I was a shy child, I was often unenthusiastic about these experiences. However, this exposure nudged me out of my comfort zone and showed me that every gift and talent could be used to spread the gospel; it was also fun to create and present with friends.

I have kept in touch with most of my classmates from NGR Sunday school, and we have often reminisced about those good old days. We still remember several of the songs and lessons from Uncle Innocent's class and have even attempted to sing the songs as adults. It is always a great time of laughter and appreciation. Several of us are active in different forms of ministry today. It is remarkable how God used one man to identify the talents and gifts in so many young people and help develop them for use in the kingdom of God. Those ribbon and bow tie-clad children from NGR were indeed equipped for a lifetime of ministry and service to God.

Kelechi Eluchie is a board-certified medical laboratory scientist. For more than a decade, she has served in various ministries, including Children's Sunday school (as a teacher), step and dance team, choir, youth ministry, women's ministry, planning and administration, finance team, health fair, and campus ministry. She is currently the president of the young adult ministry in her church in Maryland.

My talent in music was activated: Chinonso Ude (Aerospace engineer)

My name is Chinonso Ude. I am twenty-three years old, currently finishing my master's degree in aerospace engineering from the University of Maryland. I am also a gospel artist. This is a summary of how God used Uncle Innocent to impact the children's ministry at my church. Uncle Innocent Ononiwu and his family joined CAC Bethel Fellowship Church in Glendale, Maryland, when I was young. He became the teacher of the Revelation class, which was for kids between the ages of ten and thirteen years old, and under his tutelage, it quickly became the place all the kids looked forward to. Uncle Innocent made coming to church exciting for me! The first thing that comes to mind is the music we often wrote and made together, but when I set my mind to think, I remember much more.

In Uncle Innocent's class, we learned about the concept of "insight." Your "insight" represents what you learn from a passage of scripture. Often, we would be pressed to interpret scripture and communicate what we were receiving from God. Occasionally, I come across an old journal in my house, and I see old insights from class back in the day. I laugh and smile when I see that I was learning about God in a genuine way even before I really made a conscious decision to follow Him. That has been such a blessing to my life to build that habit, because now as an adult, I draw my life from that same Word that I practiced interpreting in Sunday school. That is one of the greatest gifts I have ever received from anyone.

The use of insight was multifaceted. We used our understanding to write plays, memorize scripture, compose songs, and enjoy the inherent beauty of God's Word. Looking back, it is rare that you see children in spaces where they can express themselves in those ways with *confidence*. It meant so much to me to be able to try new things all the time in Sunday school without feeling lesser than anyone or like I was being judged. I looked forward to acting in new roles and coming up with hilarious skits that helped the main point of the scriptures to come alive. I remember being one of the rascals of the class, unfortunately, and I also appreciate the discipline Uncle Innocent deployed when I was rowdy.

I will use this last portion to talk about the music. Uncle Innocent taught us to write songs based on scripture, freely expressing what we felt from it without much curating. This was a true blessing to my life that God used to stir up a gift in me. 2 Timothy 1:6 says, "For this reason, I remind you to fan into flame the gift of God, which is in you through the laying on of my hands."

This happened to me with the gift of songwriting. Uncle gave us a chance to write and perform songs together and even produced a CD of us singing together as a class. Through these experiences, I fell in love with writing songs, and over ten years later, I have continued to write songs to the glory of God. I have gone as far as recording my own music because of the passion God stirred up in me from such a young age.

God used Uncle Innocent to bless and set me on a path of destiny. I was not just entertained and babysat when I came to church. I was empowered to be who God created me to be, and for that, I say thank you, Uncle, and thank you, Lord!

Nonso is an aerospace engineer and a gospel artist.

A seedling in the hands of a gardener: Olayemi Fada-hunsi (Recent graduate of Mary Washington University)

As a young eleven-year-old child from Nigeria, the prospect of attending a new church and meeting new people was unnerving. I did not know what to expect from a group of American Nigerians, but my apprehension was quickly diminished when Uncle Innocent began teaching our class in RCCG House of Praise in Chesapeake, Virginia. The warmth and comfort I felt from the class broke the barrier during this first interaction. The acceptance of the class sparked an eagerness within me to return and be an active contributor. As the weeks progressed, I became a member of the Happiness Club, and I was ecstatic.

Singing was not an option in Dr. Ononiwu's class, and I was over the moon at this notion. In Nigeria, I was the leader of the Children's choir in my church. I had full authority over praise and worship; I felt like I held the power of ministry in my hands every time I held the microphone. Every time I sang, I felt invincible in the full armor of God. My biggest fear coming to the United States was that I would lose this incredible feeling. However, I was presented with countless opportunities to carry out my passion, and I jumped at every chance to sing. My voice would bounce off the walls as I gleefully belted high notes and melodically sang low notes. I got to hold on to my confidence whilst learning the true meaning of ministry. Uncle Innocent never failed to remind me that I was not singing for the sake of singing but in pursuit of evangelizing others and spreading the word of God.

The music workshop in Happiness Club launched my progression in ministry as we worked tirelessly to develop our talents. After maturing our gifts and perfecting our presentations through rigorous rehearsals, we would minister to the entire church, and over time, our in-church, small-scale ministrations evolved beyond our bubble. I still remember the hours on a minivan traveling to states all over the United States. Whether it was Maryland, Florida, DC, or North Carolina, the gospel of the Lord was spread, and our fruits matured.

When I think of Uncle Innocent's ministry, I reflect on how he took me as a seedling and nourished me into a fruitful blossom for Christ. There is some irony to this because one of the first lessons that has stuck with me from his youth class is the parable of the Sower, in which seeds were sown in multiple places. "Still other seed fell on good soil, where it produces a crop - a hundred, sixty or thirty times what was sown. Whoever has ears let them hear" (Matthew 13:8-9). Uncle Innocent taught me, on that day, the importance of having a well-rooted foundation. He taught us that his purpose is to plant the seeds of God's love in us so that when we are older, we will be able to bear fruits for the kingdom of God. Uncle Innocent, to me, represents the man in the parable spreading the seed all around and bringing life, growth, and meaning into it. I feel truly blessed because every seed that he instilled in me has continued to bear fruit.

Presently, I look back at the first parable that I learned, alongside the experiences I was privileged to gain, and simply smile. My deep understanding of how our talents allow us to edify God has directed the course of my life. I am constantly pushed to continue my growth in faith and multiply my fruits because of the fertile soil that I have been groomed upon. Uncle Innocent searched for the perfect soil, planted me meticulously, and fostered a lifetime of blessings.

Olayemi is a recent graduate (double major: Biology and Psychology) of The University of Mary Washington in Fredericksburg, Virginia. She and her sister Ayoola (The Fadahunsi sisters) are a powerful duet.

Mentored for Eight Years: Nosa Lawani (Student at Harvard University)

"And that from a childhood you have known the holy scriptures, which are able to make you wise unto salvation through faith which is in Christ Jesus" (2 Timothy 3:15, NKJV).

299

Insight. This is the first word that comes to my mind when I think of my eight formative years under Uncle Innocent's tutelage at RCCG House of Praise Chesapeake, Virginia. During the early stages of the church's children's Sunday school program, Dr. Ononiwu chose me (then five years old) and some other of my mates to join his class. Later the class became known as Revelation Class and was exclusively for children ages nine to twelve. Unlike many of his later students at the church, my experience with Uncle Innocent forms some of my earliest extant memories—what a blessing!

The center of every class, as I recall, was on what we called "insights." Uncle Innocent would have us read aloud the week's Bible passage or topic but would not then simply carry on teaching. Instead, with no worry for our young ages, he would give an extended period for our own quiet reflection on the Bible passage that we read. In our notebooks, we were tasked each week with writing ten original insights from the lesson. After this, we would each share and discuss one another's insights, with Uncle Innocent giving comments and guidance as we formed our own shared and original understanding of the scripture. At one point, he began to rank them with an asterisk system. I remember the joy that my competitive childhood spirit would feel at the coveted three asterisks—but this competition and joy, as I see now, was in pursuit of the truth of God. Though we were little aware of how much was taking place, Uncle Innocent was not only teaching us the Word, but how to read it, the joy of doing so, and, through God's miraculous grace in him, giving to us each our own spirit of discernment.

Then from these new, shared understandings, Uncle Innocent would have us create, we would be let outside in groups to form skits or original songs which ministered something of the day's teaching. Again, to us, this might have been simple fun, but we were being given an early opportunity to give life to the Word and thereby to see joy in the lifelong duty of those called to Christ. Through caring and exacting instruction, he equipped us with tools of ministry that live far beyond his class: singing in harmony and in time, and, when appropriate, even with a tasteful vibrato, the art of analogy in developing skits, and the confidence and skill to act out these effectively. Like insights, these activities were judged, often sternly, but with a love that sought to bring us towards excellence. He also taught us that there was fruit for this excellence beyond the class' going wild at a record 9.8/10 skit or a four-asterisk insight; a great skit would be refined, rehearsed, and finally presented during one of the church's Children's Days. An excellent insight could form the seed of a student's sermon given before the class and then, after further development, before the church (as I was the first to do). At other times, the fruit of our labors would simply be spontaneous: my siblings and I still sing, the three-part round the class song that we composed in the final minutes of one church service, "Shall We Pray?"

After my time in Happiness Club, these lessons did not leave me. I had always been a voracious reader, and, at school, my praised ability to analyze, no doubt, came from that weekly training in the Word with Uncle Innocent. So too, likely, did my joy for learning, which made me always seek things better and more excellent. Blessed with parents able and willing to support me, the seeking led me to leave Virginia at fourteen for boarding school at Phillips Exeter in New Hampshire. The school prides itself on its "unique" method of instruction, which places emphasis on student discussion rather than teacher-lecturing; what they touted, however, was what we had taken for granted for years as children in his Happiness Club.

Unlike Uncle Innocent's class, however, in this secular academic environment, we were not discussing the Word, nor did we have teachers who would guide us towards that truth. Instead, English, History, Science classes, discussions with my peers, and even social media would bring me new knowledge, but not the discernment that brings all things— be it Bible stories or American History—under the captivity of Christ. Although I continued to learn much and develop my ability to analyze, it was on the world's thorny ground. In these discussions, the devouring lion was often roaring, and

I grew confused. There was always, even while many others and even parts of me accepted these diverse teachings, something within me that fiercely sought something better, something more excellent, something true.

During this COVID-19 period, by God's providence, I spent the longest time at home than I had in four years. Seeking, I returned earnestly to the Word, with all the new knowledge and analytical skills I had added to the old and had what I can perhaps only describe as an encounter with God. After the eventful and systematic study of the gospel according to John and Genesis, I felt the reconciliation of many years of confusing knowledge. Even more so, I felt a truth that my entire self was able to believe, and from there, my faith.

I am so thankful to God that entering Harvard, I have this tested faith, which my new studies cannot combat but will only grow. I am thankful for both the tests and the testimony. And I am thankful to the man of God, who every week for eight years sowed the incorruptible seed that is the Word within me, Uncle Innocent.

Nosa is a student at Harvard University.

A changed Teenager: Abigail Musembi (A thirteen-year-old current pupil in KidsZone)

303

I will have to admit; I was not so open to the thought of having a new Faith class teacher but having this one changed my life for the better. About two years ago, Dr. Innocent was introduced to our class (Faith Class: nine to thirteen years old kids) as a new Sunday school teacher. At the time, we had Auntie Amma as our teacher. She had been our teacher for a while. So, when we heard that he would be replacing her, I was a bit disappointed.

I remember very fondly when he told us his name was Dr. Innocent, we thought that he was joking, but apparently, he was profoundly serious. I couldn't help but laugh. Never did I think I would meet someone with the name Innocent. But soon enough, I calmed myself down. We all introduced ourselves to Dr. Innocent, and since then, he has been teaching us.

I feel like the kid's department has really grown because of him becoming a teacher here. Our little choir has become a lot better, and new talents have been discovered. For example, we found out about how one of the boys in our class, Greg, could play the drums really well. And the previous summer, a bunch of us got to learn new instruments. I learned a bit of the bass guitar, and in three weeks, I was able to play along to a song. As I am writing this, we are getting prepared for our Christmas Concert. Ever since he joined us, the kid's department has gained more popularity. Last year, at the Christmas Concert, we did so well that the next Sunday, we had so many kids in the KidsZone that we had to pull extra chairs every time someone came in. It really goes to show that his help did make a difference.

For me personally, Dr. Innocent has been a blessing. If God had not sent him here, I don't know how I would be now. There was a time when we were in class, around Halloween time, some of the kids were talking about trick or treating at Halloween time. I remember him talking about how demonic Halloween is and how we should not be celebrating it. I had known that it was not the most Christian thing, but I hadn't thought too much of it. He said that Halloween is a way to lure children into the devil's trap because of the candy. And if you think about it, it is absolutely true. If there was no candy on Halloween, I am sure that it wouldn't have as much hype as it does now. But it was just little things like this that led me to take God more seriously.

Slowly but surely, having Dr. Innocent as a teacher grew me as a person. Looking at myself now and myself then, we have vastly different morals. The things I could do then, I cannot even think about doing now. This was especially important because most of us have the mindset that we, as people, do not have to learn anything because we already know enough. From having Dr. Innocent as my teacher, I learned that you can never know too much, and it is good to expand our knowledge. Even though the Faith class is learning about serious things, we always find some fun things to do. Dr. Innocent has been a real blessing to us in the kid's department.

Abby was a pupil in the Faith Class of KidsZone, RCCG York, Pennsylvania until June 2021.

12

Go in This Might of Yours

Publish it in the day, publish it at night. The Lord needs your voice

As we draw close to the end of this book, let me leave you with a charge. Do not let the seed die. In the preceding chapters, I have shared with you the challenges and dilemmas that we encounter in the children's ministry. We have systematically tried to provide guidance on how to navigate the choppy waters of ministering to children in a digital age and achieving positive results. What is left is for you to go out there and put into practice what you have gleaned from some of the experiences and testimonies that we have shared in this book. Recently I listened to two medical doctors speak on multiple streams of income during a Christian marriage seminar. Dr. Nneka Unachukwu (Dr. Una), a pediatrician and Chief Executive Officer of Ivy League Pediatrics in Norcross, Georgia, and host of the *Entremed* podcast, spoke on "your seed" while Dr. Chiagozie Fawole, a pediatric anesthesiologist and founder of Savvy-Docs real estate investment platform in Syracuse, New York spoke on "selling your oil." Dr. Una said, "Respect your seed," while Dr. Fawole counseled, "Sell the oil." Let me borrow a leaf from both doctors and ask you to respect your seed and sell the oil.

Respect your seed

Each one of us is blessed with a seed that, if planted in the right soil, will yield an oak tree of treasures in our lives, family, ministry, and community. According to Dr. Una, the seed you may have is simply "favor." If you recognize this seed, you will use it to reach another milestone in your upward journey in ministry, family life, or even your finances. One of my friends had this seed of favor. As a college student, he had difficulty paying his tuition. He was not eligible for financial aid and was working two or three jobs and going to school. Life was rough for him. However, he had favor with one official in the accounts department who allowed him to pay whatever he could whenever he had the money. Four years later, he had paid up all his tuition and graduated from the pharmacy school debt-free. That seed of favor got translated to a Doctor of Pharmacy degree (Pharm. D). Armed with a Pharm. D and a license to practice pharmacy, which now became another seed in his hand, my friend got a job with one of the big retail pharmacies in the United States. With good income as a branch manager, another seed to sow into some real estate investment, he now has multiple streams of income. The young man who was struggling to pay his tuition is now sowing the seed of favor in the lives of other people who are stranded in the life's train station of poverty in which he was stuck several years ago.

What seed do you have in your hand? Do not disparage it. Respect it. Commit it into the hands of the Lord and turn it into gold. It is possible that what you have is great leadership potential. You seem to see possibilities where others fail. Turn it on and ask the Lord how you can use it to create programs, outreaches, represent the children's ministry needs to your church leadership, and organize field trips for the children. Are you a playwright? Create scripture-based skits for kids in your church and teach them how to write and act short plays. What if your seed is in technology? Can you think of ways to make your children's Sunday school use of technology the best in your city or even your country? Can you bring the teachers in your ministry up to speed with the use of technology in the classroom? Can you develop apps that facilitate the interaction of your pupils with their teachers? Make Sunday school fun for the kids, and in turn, they will listen to and absorb the gospel message that you teach them.

When you sow your seeds at one level, prepare for the harvest that will follow and the further potentials that the harvest will generate. Your harvest will provide you multiple seeds to sow. Plan then to expand your storage facilities and distribution outlets. What I am saying, in essence, is when you yield your abilities, expertise, and social capital to the service of the Lord, He will enlarge your coast. If you are faithful in the little that you have, the Lord will give you more responsibilities. Respect your seed.

Sell your oil

During the seminar that I referred to, Dr. Fawole used the story of the widow whose creditors threatened to sell her sons to satisfy a debt that she owed them to illustrate what should happen when the Lord gives you life-changing ideas.

> Then he said, "Go, borrow vessels from everywhere, from all your neighbors—empty vessels; do not gather just a few. And when

you have come in, you shall shut the door behind you and your sons; then pour it into all those vessels and set aside the full ones. So she went from him and shut the door behind her and her sons, who brought the vessels to her; and she poured it out. Now it came to pass, when the vessels were full, that she said to her son, "Bring me another vessel."And he said to her, "There is not another vessel." So the oil ceased. Then she came and told the man of God. And he said, "Go, sell the oil and pay your debt; and you and your sons live on the rest.

2 Kings 4: 3-7 (NKJV)

According to her, the miracle that God performed through Elisha by filling the widow's borrowed vessels with oil would have amounted to nothing if the woman failed to sell the oil. Often, we ask the Lord to give us life-changing ideas but stop short of selling them when he does. The Sunday school model that we use today has been long overdue for overhaul. Is God giving you ideas on how best to change the approach to yield more positive outcomes? Share the ideas. Publish them. Do not go to the grave with your beautiful ideas. Write books, start a blog, post something on

Facebook or other social media platforms that will generate discussions, challenge the status quo, share links that will help other teachers locate valuable information that will enrich their ministry. Create Bible clubs and use what tools you have in your hands to move your children's ministry forward. Over the years, I have used my gifts in writing and producing plays, songs, and poems to add value to the lives of the children in our children's ministry. By God's grace, I am doing my little part to communicate what worked in our ministry in this book. If you have read up to this page, congratulations. You have information that you can turn into gold. This is one more thing you can do to propagate this message. Share copies of this book with the teachers and parents and encourage them to share with their contacts on social media platforms. Let us put one million copies in the hands of children's ministry workers worldwide in one year. In Psalm 68:11, the scripture says, "The Lord gave the word; Great was the company of those who published it" (KJV).

Here is the information that the Lord is passing on to you through this book. Will you commit to passing it on to at least ten more people? We are in the digital age. There are many ways you can make this message go viral. You may write a commentary or a brief review and post on your social media or help draw the attention of others to this book. Either way, you are doing the Lord's work and improving our Sunday schools and children's ministries. Go in this might of yours. Go sell your oil. Do not let the seed die.

Appendix One

Other resources

Here are some useful internet resources that can enrich your children's ministry experience:

1. Bible App for Kids. This is a free App that presents interactive and animated Bible stories that kids can watch on tablets or computers. https://play.google.com/store/apps/details?id=com.bible.kids&hl=en_US&gl=US

2. Superbook Bible for Kids from Christian Broadcasting Network (CBN) is available on the CBN website. It is a creative animation of Bible stories. https://www.cbn.com/superbook/

3. Lifeway Kids from Lifeway Christian Resources. https://www.lifeway.com/en/shop/ministries/kids

4. Play Bible Trivia from RD Games Inc. Specifically created to make God's word relevant and entertaining. https://www.playthebible.com/download-play-the-bible-for-android/

5. Bible Word Puzzle from iDailyBread: Creative and

animated fun Bible games with fun quizzes. https://appgrooves.com/app/bible-word-puzzle-by-idaily-bread-co-limited

6. Bible jeopardy game. https://www.christianity.com/trivia/jeopardy/

7. Child Evangelism Fellowship: The Child Evangelism Fellowship has a lot of ministry resources on its website. https://www.cefonline.com/

8. Children Evangelism Ministry: Several ministry materials are available on their website. https://www.ceminternational.org/

9. Kids in Ministry: Good materials on redefining children's ministry can be found on their website. http://kidsinministry.org/

Appendix Two

Sample of the comprehension exercise worksheet:

KidsZone: Worksheeet # 21

FAITH CLASS

TEACHER FOR THE DAY:_____

YOUR NAME:_____

Topic: Practical Christianity series: Ask God for Wisdom

Texts for The Day: James 1: 1-8

Power Text (Memory verse): James 1:5

Answer the following questions.

1) What does the scripture you read suggest that you do when you need wisdom? _____

_____

_____

2) What will God do when you ask Him for wisdom? __

_____

_____

_____

3) What does wisdom mean? _____

_____

_____

_____

_____

4) How are we supposed to ask God for wisdom? _____

_____

_____

5) Write down 5 insights from the passage you read

A. _____

_____

B. _____

_____

C. _____

_____

D. _____

_____

E. _____

Parent's Signature _____

Teacher's Signature _____

Appendix Three

A sample of an insight by one of my pupils (eleven years old):

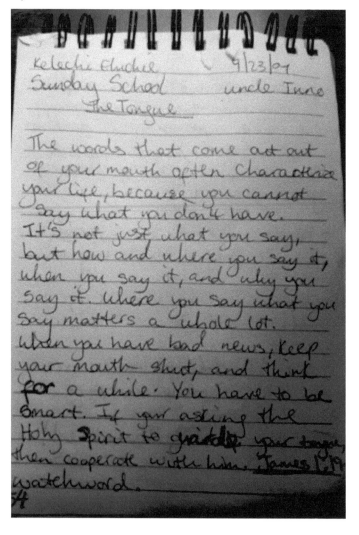

About the Author

Dr. Innocent Maduabughichukwu Ononiwu is a pharmacist and holds a PhD in Pharmacology. For more than thirty-three years, Dr. Ononiwu taught Pharmacology and conducted drug discovery research in pharmacy and medical schools both in Nigeria and the United States of America.

He is best known for the work he has been doing with children. Uncle Innocent (as he is fondly called) has been a children's Sunday school teacher from 1972 to the present. He has served as a children's Sunday school teacher or co-ordinator in seven cities in Africa and the United States of America. He is currently the coordinator of the children's department (KidsZone) in RCCG York in Pennsylvania. When the famous Happiness Club was started in 1980 for children at the University of Ife in Nigeria, Innocent was invited to participate as one of the founding instructors. The other two founding instructors, Obiora and Nath, left the university after graduating from the institution and Innocent carried on with the vision. He and his wife, Vickie, nurtured the club to national prominence. They also established similar activity groups in the University of Port-Harcourt in Nigeria, Bethel Fellowship Church in Glendale (Maryland), RCCG House of Praise in Chesapeake (Virginia), and RCCG Living Spring in York (Pennsylvania).

Dr. Ononiwu is a poet, playwright, actor, singer, and songwriter. He has written about one hundred poems and forty-five inspirational thoughts. He has also written more than 200 songs with his wife, Vickie, produced two albums of their original songs and one video documentary with Happiness Club. Since 2006, Dr. Ononiwu has been organizing annual summer music workshops for children during which children with musical talents are discovered and trained in several musical instruments. He also conducts voice training for children during the workshops.

He was the founding coordinator of Ebony Productions, a Christian organization founded in 1996 which produces an annual Christian Easter concert called Bubble (Now in its 24th season) in Port-Harcourt, Nigeria. In 1986 he founded a youth outreach program in All Souls Chapel University of Ife, also called Bubble, which provides a platform for the youth and young adults to reach out to their peers under the supervision of adult teachers.

Innocent is the author of two books on marriage (*Jewels for my dear wife* and *Diamonds and roses*). He also authored the autobiographical book *God knows my house number* and is currently working on books for children and inspirational thoughts. He has written scripts and produced children's Christmas concerts, including *The Lion became the Lamb, Messiah: Great news,* and *Wings of joy.* He is the head of the Marriage and Family Ministry in RCCG York and is a speaker in Christian marriage and children's ministry seminars and workshops.

Dr. Innocent Ononiwu is married with five children and currently has three grandchildren.